UP WITH AUTHORITY

UP WITH AUTHORITY

Why We Need Authority to Flourish as Human Beings

VICTOR LEE AUSTIN

t&t clark

Published by T&T Clark International
A Continuum Imprint

The Tower Building
11 York Road
London SE1 7NX

80 Maiden Lane
Suite 704
New York NY 10038

www.continuumbooks.com

British Library Cataloguing-in-Publication Data
A catalogue record for this book is available from the British Library.

ISBN: 978-0-567-30809-2 (Hardback)
978-0-567-02051-2 (Paperback)

Typeset by Newgen Imaging Systems Pvt Ltd, Chennai, India
Printed and bound in the United States of America

To
the Reverend Andrew C. Mead
and
the People of Saint Thomas Church

CONTENTS

ACKNOWLEDGMENTS

In this book I argue that we humans are essentially social beings all the way to the end. So in a profound sense I feel gratitude to all my teachers, friends, and colleagues, not to mention wife, children, parents, and in-laws, who have given me opportunity to see how much I am connected with them.

Several of my friends succumbed to my importuning them to read portions, and sometimes all, of this manuscript: John Van Doren, Stephen Hildebrand, Susan Ironside, Ron Mawby, R. R. Reno, John Scott, Daron Vroon, and Jeremy Waldron. I am grateful for their insights and have tried to learn from them. And I hope that once they see how far I have fallen short, I will not have to reckon them as former friends.

This book began as a paper presented at the annual conference of the Society of Christian Ethics in Atlanta in 2008. My gratitude extends to the participants in my section and to the two anonymous reviewers of my paper.

As it does to the Church Club of New York, who invited me to speak with them about authority in the church. Portions of that address have also made it into this book.

Drafts of the chapters of this book were read to adult theology classes at Saint Thomas Church, where I am theologian-in-residence. We had many lively conversations, which helped me become clearer about the dimensions of this matter of authority. Again, my thanks.

Above all, I give thanks to and for the Reverend Andrew C. Mead, rector of Saint Thomas Church in New York City. Father Mead's distinguished career in the Episcopal Church has been marked throughout by the seriousness with which he takes doctrine and theological formation. That he would call me to be the parish's first theologian-in-residence is for me a source of great joy.

Saint Thomas Church Fifth Avenue
December 1, 2009

Chapter 1

INTRODUCTION: WE CAN'T GET ALONG WITHOUT IT

To Succeed at Being a Human Being

The point of this book is to show that we need authority to be ourselves. We cannot succeed at being human beings—we cannot have a flourishing human life—without the functioning of authority in the multiple dimensions within which we live. I will try to demonstrate this reality in four fundamental dimensions of human life that pertain to freedom, truth, power, and God. And I will be arguing that this necessity of authority does not come upon us because of some tragic flaw in human beings. Rather, the necessity of authority is a manifestation of the glory of being human.

When we speak about being human, theology offers us a narrative that runs something like this. First off, human beings were made. Then there was a tragic event whereby they "fell" from their original state. God, however, did not desire to leave humans in sin, so he introduced means for them to rise above sin and be restored to a fullness of being. Thus the basic narrative has three significant points: creation, fall, and redemption. In the Christian version, the final point of the narrative itself divides: there is the redemption accomplished by Christ's death and resurrection, but there is also, still to come, a final restoration of all things in God's ultimate judgment.

Now ask yourself: where should authority be placed in this theological narrative of the human being? Many people would place it *between the fall and the redemption*, and they would give an account something like the following. When God created human beings, they were free and perfect, if innocent, and they had no need of authority to guide them. It is only because we are sinners, according to this view, that we need authority. Authority comes into the picture because (and only because) the human being fails to be a complete or full or perfect human being. But imagine that we were otherwise than, in fact, we are. Imagine, this view says, that the human being had no sin, and thus no wrongful self-centeredness, no inclination toward unfairness, no desire to carry on a history of vengeful retaliation, and so forth. If we were perfect, this view says, we should no longer need authority. Theologically speaking, this view puts authority into the narrative space that comes after the fall and prior to the (final) redemption.

I think the clearest way to state the difference of my view from the foregoing is to say that this book places authority *all through the narrative.* My argument will be that even "perfect" human beings need authority. In fact, the argument goes so far as to say that unsinful human beings need authority *even more than* sinners. Authority is built into what it means to be human, and we never will escape from needing it for our flourishing.

Chapters 2 through 5 make this argument with regard to society, epistemology (how we know the truth), politics, and the church. In each case, the argument is both that we as flawed human beings need authority, and that as we become less flawed (what I call "more human," on the assumption that we can grow or diminish in life and thus become more fully human, or less) we will need authority all the more. Thus I argue in Chapter 2 that, contrary to what we might unthinkingly assume, authority is positively related to freedom: as we become more free, we need more authority. This claim correlates closely with the claim that human nature is ineluctably social. Then in Chapter 3 I argue that authority is also positively related to knowledge of the truth. For it is the case that we always know more than we can say. And it is epistemic authority that accounts for how our knowledge is greater than what reason can deliver.

I turn to political authority in Chapter 4. Many people would start (and end) their discussion of authority with politics. But politics involves, when we deal with sinful persons, the potential exercise of coercive force. And it is helpful to see that authority, in its social and epistemic modes, is quite distinct from coercive force; and that, even in politics, coercion comes with authority only because of sin and then only at the boundaries. In Chapter 4 the reader will find a theological account of political authority as the coordination in a single agency of power, judgment, and the preservation of tradition. There is no political authority when there is no power to carry out judgment or to preserve and carry forward the identity of a people.

Authority in the church, the subject of Chapter 5, is a different matter. Here I take up the question of the authority of Scripture and the authority of church structures and rites. When authority is discussed in ecumenical settings, Scripture, rites, and authority-persons (bishops, popes) are the neuralgic points. But the burden of the chapter is to show that authority in the church becomes actualized in the individual believer; the authorized person is the one who truly confesses Christ in word and deed, and it is to her that we should look to understand ecclesiastical authority, the relation of authority to God. From authority in the church, thus seen, we can return to the earlier chapters and see more clearly what was only obscure earlier: that, for instance, social authority fulfills itself in the free actions of persons in society, and that political authority can be embodied and carried in an individual who lacks authorization to judge and perpetuate tradition officially.

So authority is necessary in all these fundamental dimensions of human life. Nonetheless, it is no part of my argument to claim that authority is always right. Authorities can and do err, all the time, in all these dimensions: society, epistemology, politics, and the church. How can we live with this dual reality that we need authority in order to flourish and, nonetheless, there is no guarantee that authority is correct in any given instance? That is the subject of Chapter 6.

From Chapter 2 onward this book argues that authority is a performative concept. By that I mean it is something that is real when it is in action, being "performed." We may call Sandra an authority on the snakes of Louisiana, but she is truly such only when she is engaged in scholarly-scientific activity related to the apprehension of herpetological truth. We may think of Antonio as a political authority even when he is asleep, but he is truly such when he is providing judgment. Or Bill, a baptized Christian, is an authority when he claims for himself the Christian profession and works accordingly in society. We speak of scholarly snake monographs, judicial institutions, and Christian creeds as having authority, but that authority really exists only in a person who is doing what authorities do.

Which is, to provide what is needed for human beings to flourish. For this reason, I found it necessary that this book end in heaven. Following Dante (who was following Beatrice, who was following Love), I suggest in Chapter 7 that even in paradise we will not find ourselves beyond authority. Rather, since authority exists within God's own being, redeemed humanity will be forever *within* authority.

Why it Matters that We Value Authority

The reader will have seen already that this book is a work against the stream. Unavoidably, each of us carries around a body of cultural assumptions, myriad unarticulated suppositions that we take, without examination, as truths. I will argue strongly that we cannot do without suppositions that we take as true. Unfortunately, with regard to authority, many currently regnant assumptions are false. It matters that we, counter-culturally, start to question these assumptions. You may have been taught—I was; it's one of the earliest bumper stickers I can remember—to "Question Authority." This book, then, is an invitation to go beyond that bumper-sticker slogan, to question the notion that authority is intrinsically questionable.

From several years of giving talks on authority, I have had opportunity to learn many of the objections people bring to an argument that authority has a needed and positive role for human flourishing. Indeed, some of these may have occurred already to you.

The Bible does not have a positive view of authority. For instance, at Mk 10.42 Jesus says to his disciples, "You know that those who are supposed to rule over the Gentiles lord it over them, and their great men exercise authority over them."[1] Here, to "exercise authority" is to "lord it over," and, as the next verse says, it is not supposed to be that way among the disciples of Jesus. According to this objection, authority is not something that should characterize human beings when they are in a godly society.

A similar point is made by *libertarians.* Human beings have problems when they are not trusted to act freely. And so the solution to human problems lies in maximizing liberty by minimizing authority. We need governments that are as small as possible, so that we can be as free as possible. And we need, in general, to prioritize the individual over society, so that we are free of social conventions, lock-step thinking, and the like. The more is granted to societies (of any sort, even neighborhoods and families), the greater the harm to the flourishing of the human individual. Human maturity is the growth of human

1 This quotation is from the King James Version, which I often use in appreciation of its cultural resonances for English-speaking people. In Anglican churches it is traditionally known as the Authorized Version, a usage that I continue on occasion. All unattributed biblical quotations in this book are from the King James, or Authorized, Version. For clarity or other purposes I sometimes use the New Revised Standard Version (NRSV)—and in such instances the translation being quoted is identified.

individuality, the throwing away of the shackles of conformity, the stepping free of all authority.

And from the opposing political side we find a similar critique of authority. Under *socialist* analysis, the blame for human want rests on capitalist structures. It is the power of the free market, the authority exercised by capitalists, that needs to be overthrown. By extrapolation, this critical school of argument has identified structures of oppression in matters of race, gender, and class. The authority of these received structures needs to be questioned and undermined, so that human beings can rise up free from racism, sexism, and classism into an egalitarian future of the flourishing of all people.

Furthermore, *technological advance*, which has brought innumerable benefits to human beings and enabled them to flourish to an extent hitherto unimaginable—those very technological advances have gone hand-in-hand with the diminishment and overthrowing of authority. And there is an easily-grasped reason for this. To discover a new technology requires that one be willing to question the received wisdom about how a particular matter should be done. Proponents of this argument would have us look at the place where technological advances occur. For the most part (it may be said), they do not arise within the walls of established institutions, but rather on the periphery, where small entrepreneurs work to discover the next new thing. It is not under authority that new discoveries are made, but outside authority. Authority, according to this objection, oppresses novelty and innovation.

These four objections to authority are, as I said, commonly made: authority is ungodly; it is anti-individual; it props up established power structures; and it resists change. But let me propose to you some illustrations that, I believe, suggest a contrary view. Like the former, these illustrations point to aspects of our contemporary world. Yet, if you attend to them carefully, you may pick up a hint of what authority is good for.

For the two decades that I lived in New York's Hudson Valley, the village of Woodstock was a place my family liked to visit. It is a quaint, walkable town, with coffee shops, antiques, bookstores, farmer stands, and in general a lot of character. It is also, of course, the place that gave its name to the 1969 festival that, iconically, stands for cultural rebellion against received authority. Although our visits to Woodstock were pleasant, and it is a place for which I feel a certain affinity (my wife has pictures of me with shoulder-length hair, which we try to hide from the children), nonetheless I could not suppress a certain sense of loss, there in the presence of a number of aging, grey-haired hippies. What happens, I thought, when those who rebel against the authority of age, themselves become aged? What is it like to rebel against authority—and then go on to live another 20, 30, 40 years? This, of course, is a question about much more than a small village in New York (which, anyway, was not the location of the 1969 festival which took its name). It is a question about our much-remarked cultural fixation on youth. We can acknowledge that youth-idolization is illusory and harmful to real human beings; but do we often see the link between those illusions and harms and the rejection of authority that goes with the celebration of youth culture?

Consider, too, the transmission of customs and practices that help us live together. Authority is necessarily involved in the transmission of customs and practices, and accordingly the attempt to reject authority is often manifested in the rejection of customs and practices. Are we unquestionably better off having rejected them? I will mention some things that are almost trivial. My generation, I believe, was the last to be trained in handwriting (which is not to say that mine is any good). I failed to be trained in urbane manners of speech, although I was enculturated to certain manners at the table. It seems to me there is a value in received customs such as handwriting and courteous speech that we may appreciate only retrospectively, after they have passed from the scene. We recognize civility in our social life only after civil customs have gone. At the time of my childhood education, I thought of such tokens of civility as nothing but burdensome customs, and I bristled under their transmission. But what else might be thought of as burdensome customs? Reliability? Truth-telling? I am glad that the man who sells me life insurance does not consider truth-telling a burdensome custom, even though his integrity has diminished his short-term profits. But would I even notice his integrity if it were not for a broader failure of authoritative cultural transmission, the incivility that characterizes much of our social life?

It is true, as one of the objections said above, that technology undermines authority. And technology has benefited humans in many ways. Nonetheless, it is clearly not true that technology advances hand-in-hand with advances in human flourishing. Here is an off-beat example. Thanks to the technology of digital video cameras, computers, and the Internet, it is now possible to attempt to teach yourself ballet at home. And many are trying to do so. "Web videos are shaking loose the rigid hierarchy of the ballet world," according to the *Wall Street Journal*. This would seem to be a clear example of technology undermining a structure of authority ("the rigid hierarchy of the ballet world") and allowing many more people to flourish as dancers. But it goes quickly awry. It seems there are many things in ballet that you can't pick up on your own, for which you need a teacher's guidance and example. Without that guidance, the price paid can be severe. "'The person who teaches themselves how to dance *en pointe* has a fool for a dance teacher,' says a New York orthopedic surgeon."[2]

A final example. In 1989 the diocese of New York in the Episcopal Church was preparing to elect a bishop. There were meetings to survey the views of people on what we wanted in our next bishop. In a day-long workshop, it was repeatedly stated that we wanted a bishop who would listen to us, embrace a diversity of persons and views, and be an enabler of our various ministries. It was explicitly said that we did not want a hierarchical bishop. Absent from those conversations was the thought that authority could be both substantive and beneficial. Are we indeed well-served by "leaders" who stand for nothing except fair process (and who thus cannot "lead")? In fact, people often suspect that processes are stacked in advance so as to generate the result that the non-leader-who-just-stands-for-fair-process person can get the result he wanted all along. It seems to me a sign of our cultural impoverishment that we lack a notion of authorities who have *something to convey to us*, have *a place to lead us toward*, authorities, that is, who embody a sense of what the human good is and who exist to help us flourish in it.

Many other examples could be offered. I offer these four to the reader as signs in our world that authority belongs to human flourishing: the wasteland that can follow the rejection of authority; our sense of the diminishment of civility in social life; the reflection that technology need not be positively related to human flourishing and can lead to human harm; and the loss that we live with when we have managers rather than leaders. At the time of that diocesan gathering, I told my friends I was going to start sporting a lapel button that read "Up with Hierarchy." That would have been good ironic fun, but I now see that the issue isn't in hierarchy. Hierarchy is but one possible structuring of authority. Had I a button today, it would read "Up with Authority."

2 "On Their Toes and Asking for Trouble, Self-Taught Ballerinas Go Online," *Wall Street Journal*, June 3, 2008, A1, A18.

After Authority

Up with Authority is the work of a philosophically-minded theologian who is curious about how it is that we humans live together. It seems to me that people in our time are trying to live without authority. There used to be authority, but (we think) we have outgrown it; so that our world is *after* (i.e., "post") authority. But also, since I am convinced that authority is necessary to our living together well, this book is an essay that is "after" authority in the sense of "going after" or "trying to grasp." In a sense, this book is my small homage to Alisdair MacIntyre's *After Virtue*, whose cultural-intellectual critique was that we in the West had lost our grasp on the meaning and centrality of the virtues to ethics, and whose book set out after their reclamation.[3] Like MacIntyre in the face of intractable ethical debates, I am frustrated by the seeming endlessness with which we go on about political matters and church matters, debates that for all their incessant quality never achieve depth of understanding. Is there something worth knowing about ourselves that would make politics a dignified activity? Can we have integrity in our lives, so that we understand and think consistently from the pronouncements of a court to the preservation of an intellectual tradition to the hope of eternal life?

This book is theologically grounded. When I hang out my shingle, the word on it is "theologian." But I am also a priest in the Episcopal Church, which has placed me in a variety of situations in which I have had pastoral and educational opportunities. I have taught college courses in ethics and theology in settings from small and rural to urban and sophisticated, and I have taught at seminary. So I have often had to face the question of how theology connects with everyday life, in lots of different kinds of everyday life. And I have often wondered about the connections of things—of math and theology, for instance, or symphony conductors and prime ministers.

This book is the product of me trying to think through the question of authority. It does not aim to smother the subject with a survey of what everyone has said, although certain writers on authority have helped me think, and I will introduce them to you in these pages. The book is more essay than dissertation, a "raid on the inarticulate" rather than a

3 Alisdair MacIntyre, *After Virtue*, 3rd ed. (Notre Dame: University of Notre Dame Press, 2007).

comprehensive treatment. My interlocutors come from various fields: philosophers, theologians, ecclesiastics, and even a poet. Principally they include Yves Simon, Michael Polanyi, Oliver O'Donovan, Richard Hooker, the Anglican-Roman Catholic International Commission, and Dante Alighieri. But my purpose throughout has been not to give the definitive account of, say, Simon on social authority, but rather to learn from Simon more about social authority. Yes, this book will help acquaint the reader with Simon, Polanyi, O'Donovan, and others. But its purpose is to bring the reader to a better understanding of authority: that it is forever a part of human flourishing, and that that is good news.

Where Does Authority Come From?

I will claim that the human being is essentially social, and that this means, for us, that the group pre-exists the individual. A consequence of this view is that authority is not something that we construct. Rather, authority is *already there* in the world around us within which we come to be as humans.

In the terms of theology, we may speak of authority as an aspect of God's providence for the human race. It's as if we come awake one day to the reality that we live in a governed society, and we see the good that such government provides for us (even as, at the same time, we may realize the government's shortcomings). My family may fall short of what a family should be, but insofar as it is still a "family," it is a social provision from which I derive some potentiality for flourishing. My church, the local ballet company, the corporate office across the street: these and untold other human groupings existed before I came along and all have contributed to the possibilities for me as a human. As I mature (which is to say, in the process of my flourishing to whatever extent it comes about), I will in turn have an impact on society, epistemology, politics, and the church. So I may have an effect on authorities; I may even become an authority. But authority was there before I came along.

Authority, that is to say, is not a product of consensus—an argument to which I will often return in the pages that follow. But, interestingly, this is not to say that authority has nothing to do with consent. The Great Books scholar John Van Doren has pointed out that consent is neither consensus nor agreement but "what the mind sees, or may see, when it understands."[4] Consent is what happens when we think together. Reason can guide us to consent to an argument, but consent extends beyond the deliverances of reason.

So here is our first statement of the paradox that is authority. Authority has to do with our understanding (our consent), and yet it was there before we began to think about it.

A Few Words Up Front About the Acceptance of Paradox

Since we have thus run into it, it will be helpful to conclude this introductory chapter by saying something about paradox.

In my early days of trying to think like a Christian I was much taken by the line, attributed to Tertullian, a father of the early church: "I believe *because* it is absurd!" Tertullian was referring to the central claims of Christian faith. I was wrestling with the doctrine of the Incarnation of the Son of God, namely, that the Word of God took on flesh and became fully human without ceasing in any way to be divine. But I should have noticed that Tertullian is not called "Saint Tertullian." Some more seasoned Christians tried to warn me off this celebration of contradiction; my St. John's College seminar tutor gently asked if I truly wanted to elide the difference between contradiction and paradox. Impatiently I did just that, and produced a sophomore paper on the Incarnation that celebrated God becoming man precisely because, I said, it was a contradiction to be God and man at the same time.

But in truth there is a difference between contradiction and paradox, and if we can grasp the difference we will find many things, and not just theological things, to be easier to understand. A contradiction is something which simply cannot exist; it is the simultaneous assertion of "X" and "not-X" in the exact same sense. It is a contradiction to say that an object is a circle and a square in exactly the same sense. Such an object cannot exist. It is a contradiction to say that Fred is a man and a duck in exactly the same sense. Such a Fred cannot exist. We can

4 Private correspondence with the author. For an insightful essay on what it means for government to derive its just powers from the "consent" of the governed, see Scott Buchanan, "So Reason Can Rule: The Constitution Revisited," in *idem, So Reason Can Rule* (New York: Farrar, Straus, Giroux, 1982), 185–228. I am grateful to John Van Doren for leading a seminar in which we discussed this essay.

imagine a stubby cylinder which we look at from the round end: in that sense, a cylinder would be a circle; it could cast a circular shadow. But move to the side, and the stubby cylinder might look like a square and cast a square shadow. So in different senses, in fact from different perspectives, one object might be both a circle and a square. But a circle can never be a square, plain and simple.

Similarly, an experimental scientist might mix together the genetic elements that go to make up a duck with those that go to make up a human; the result, which we might call "Fred," would be part-duck and part-man. But he wouldn't be duck and man in the same sense; he wouldn't be fully a duck and fully a man. So it would not be a contradiction to say Fred was both a duck and a man, for the reason that Fred wouldn't fully be either of the two.

Contradictions cannot exist. But paradoxes can exist, and in fact many of them do. What we mean when we say something is a paradox is that we have reason to believe that some state of affairs exists which, nonetheless, we are not able fully to grasp. A paradox may look like a contradiction, but upon examination one can find reason to hold that it is not such, however puzzling it may remain. Let me give you two rather ordinary examples.

At an early point in mathematics one grasps that the whole is greater than the part. This truth is a common notion placed at the beginning of Euclid's *Elements*, one of the earliest treatments of the subject. But it turns out that for certain unlimited sets of numbers, it is not true. This is not hard to see. Compare the natural numbers (1, 2, 3, . . .) with the evens (2, 4, 6, . . .). The natural numbers make up a "whole" of which the even numbers are just a "part." In fact, that's how you could construct the second set: take the natural numbers and throw away every other number, starting with the first. Since we threw away half of them, we might think there were twice as many natural numbers as even natural numbers. Nonetheless—and this is the paradox—there are no more natural numbers than there are even natural numbers. This can be proven by the simple procedure of pairing up the nth member of the first with the nth member of the second, thus: (1, 2), (2, 4), (3, 6), and so on, where in each pair the first number comes from the natural numbers and the second number is the corresponding element in the series of even numbers. So the paradox is as follows. We have reason to say that there are no more natural numbers than even natural numbers, despite the fact that every member of the even numbers is among the natural numbers, and that half of the natural numbers (the odd ones) are not among the even numbers.

This is a paradox and not a contradiction. Mathematicians work with these "infinite" sets all day long and never come across a contradiction. They never end up saying "two equals three" or "a square is a circle" or "Fred is a duck and a man." Which is to say, for mathematicians, paradox is a very ordinary thing. Every day they go to work and play around with these infinite sets of natural numbers that have this peculiar paradoxical quality, and nothing bad happens to them. Their equations continue to work. Their paychecks keep coming in. They have learned to live with paradox.

The same story could be told of the character of light. Scientific experiments have shown that light is transmitted in tiny packets. Think of an itsy-bitsy B-B gun firing very fast: light is like that. But scientific experiments have also shown that light is transmitted like a wave. Think of the ripples on the surface of a lake when you plop a rock in it. It is impossible for us to grasp something that is at once both a particle (i.e., discontinuous) and a wave (i.e., continuous). But physicists go to work every day. They pull out their fancy equations which account for the phenomena of light, and they work with them, and everything is fine. They get their paychecks too. It is a paradox they work with: light exhibits behavior which it is flat impossible for anyone to "picture." But it is real, and the equations work, and they never have to tell their boss, "By the way, a circle is a square (and Fred is a duck)." Light is a paradox, not a contradiction.

Etymologically, a sophomore is, of course, a wise moron. My unexamined assumption as a sophomore is what I now think of as the moron-part of my nascent Christian *sophia* (wisdom). To put it briefly, my mistaken assumption was to think of God as if he were a being with a nature, a person who could be set alongside one of his creatures and, as it were, counted. But if God is the creator, then God is not a being-amongst-beings. He is the reason why we continue in being, so in that sense he is intimately close to us. But God is never alongside us in the sense that we might count him. As Herbert McCabe says, God plus the universe do not make "two."

A young person gave me a cartoon when I was ordained a priest. It was from the old "Far Side" cartoons which always delight with their signature wackiness. As I recall it,[5] there is a very unhappy, small, sweating man behind a game-show podium on which is the number zero. Beside him is his fellow contestant, a large white man in white robe with wild white hair; on his podium is a huge number in the millions.

5 The Internet has assisted my memory in reconstructing the caption.

The host of the game show is saying something like, "Yes, the answer is 'Wisconsin'! Another 500 points for God, and... uh-oh, looks like Norman, our current champion, hasn't even scored yet."

We enjoy such cartoons, and I rather enjoyed the Tertullian *frisson* of relishing the absurd. But we also know God is not a large white man who would clobber any other game-show contestant. God is not a being (amongst beings), but the cause of all beings. God is the cause of Norman's existence. God is also the cause of the game show's existence, at least insofar as the game show is a real thing. God is the cause of the existence of the strange man who invented the Far Side cartoons. God is the cause of the paper on which the cartoon, given to me, was printed. God is the cause of this book that you are holding in your hands.

When Christians say that Jesus is, at one and the same time and without equivocation, man and God, they are not saying something like "Fred is a man and a duck." Because, whatever "God" means, it cannot mean a created thing. The moronic part of my sophomore essay was that I was treating God as, in effect, a very large duck. Since God is no created thing, the Incarnation is not the contradiction that is entailed in saying something is at once "X" and "not-X" in the exact same sense. Christians do not say that Jesus is a person with two *created* natures, one human and the other not human. *We cannot understand what it means for Jesus to be at once fully God and fully man, but we can see why we are not thereby asserting a contradiction.* The Incarnation, which is beyond any mental grasp, is a paradox.

Much of this book is an implicit argument that human maturity entails the acceptance of paradox. It would be childish, if not downright stupid, to deny mathematicians their paradoxical infinities. It would be foolish to hold back from asserting that light behaves paradoxically. And it would reveal an ignorance of the radical meaning of "creation" to say that it is impossible, for the reason that it would be a contradiction, for the creator to take on flesh and become a human being. In math and science and theology, paradox commonly appears. It also appears when we consider the question of authority. Maturity requires an appropriation of paradox, which means cognition's realization that our human reality is more complex than reason can grasp. It points us to the paradoxical truth about authority, that we can't get along without it.

Chapter 2

AUTHORITY AND FREEDOM: SOCIAL AUTHORITY

Is Authority Merely Substitutionary?

Authority is something we experience every day, but is it necessary? At first we might think it not, that we have authority only when we need it to compensate for some human defect. So children need authority, as do other persons whose capacities are curtailed by handicap or unfortunate circumstance. Parents or guardians are the necessary authorities who act on their behalf. But children in the normal process of development acquire by steps or gradations their own autonomy and thus by stages free themselves from their parents. And it is a wise parent who allows the child to do so. Parental authority is temporally limited, which suggests that authority is something that *fills in when maturity is lacking*. Authority, thus, may help a child become a free human being, but freedom is precisely the autonomy that results from the diminishment and ultimate disappearance of the parent as an authority.

Parental authority is thus substitutionary. We see substitutionary authority also when we consider human sinfulness. Authority is needed to counteract our built-in egoism, our preference for our own good over another's, and to counteract indeed the injustices that we would carry out were we not opposed by countervailing authority. Consider the fact that we have law enforcement personnel. Without them, human selfishness (exhibited, for instance, behind a steering wheel) would lead to chaos. Authority steps in with its speeding tickets and liability judgments to make up for the lack in us of a good will. Thus again authority seems to work against personal freedom, although under this consideration it is the freedom to sin and prefer my own good over that of others. One might wonder what would happen if human beings were not sinful and self-centered, if they calmly considered matters from an objective point of view. Would authority then be necessary? If there were no burglars, would we need police?

Again it seems not. Thus many people deem authority to be something that we have because we fall short of being fully human, both because we (or some of us) lack adult maturity and because we (all of us) partake of the deformation of our character that is called sin. But if we were all grown-up, and none of us were handicapped or otherwise compromised in our mental and physical health, and if our sinfulness were taken away: then, we think, we would not need authority. Authority would disappear like the vanishing mist at the start of a new day.

This view, I am persuaded, is wrong. The substitutionary aspect of authority does not take us to its essence. But to perceive the essence of authority entails at the same time that we see better what freedom is—and what being human is. I am persuaded that the freer we become as human beings, the more we will need authority. This chapter intends to show what may seem paradoxical: that true authority and human freedom increase together. As an example of the positive correlation of freedom and authority, I take a symphony orchestra.

Illustration: A Symphony Orchestra

A symphony orchestra is a gathering of human beings for the purpose of performing music. It is an organization, a mini-society within a larger society. It may have a corporate identity; in the United States, it will probably be a non-profit organization operating under given laws. It likely has employees, a public that is interested in hearing its music, benefactors, officers, and the like. I will call such a society a "mini-society."

No human being belongs to just one mini-society. The people associated with the symphony will be members also of other organizations. Some of them will belong to families. Some will have employment within corporations or businesses in the same overarching community. Some will belong to churches, synagogues, mosques, or other temples. Some will participate in neighborhood groups and service organizations. Thus the simplest sort of observation shows us that to be a human is to be a member at once of a multiplicity of societies that are nested and interrelated with each other in complex ways.

When we consider a mini-society such as a symphony we abstract from certain complicating factors, setting them aside for consideration in future chapters. A symphony is not a political society, which means it lacks recourse to coercive force. It can call in the police; it can bring suit in court; but it has itself neither cop nor judge. Furthermore, a symphony is not a church. It does not then press upon us questions of ultimate truth or putative divine authority. Such questions will occupy us later. Here, by considering what happens as a symphony performs, we can isolate (more or less) the relationship of society and authority. How does authority work in the society that is a symphony orchestra?

It will be helpful to bracket out the substitutionary functions of authority that we have already identified. Let us assume that the musicians in our orchestra are competent, mature players who have graduated from "music school" (in whatever form that may have taken for them) and are quite capable of performing their repertoire expertly. Let us also assume that the musicians are selfless and committed fully to the orchestra. They are not going to carry grudges; nor will they try to undercut one another; nor will they seek more glamour for themselves than their part in the music warrants. Without sanction from contract requirements or other foreseeable penalty, they will give themselves to earnest practice so that they are always at the top of their ability, able to perform at their best. The question is: would such a symphony, composed of mature musicians free from the weight of sin, need authority?

The answer is obvious. They do need authority; they need, for starters, a conductor. This is because, with any given piece of music, there is a range of legitimate interpretations. Decisions must be made about phrasings, about tempo, about volume and blend of various instruments. On each of these questions there are many wrong answers; but there is also seldom just one right answer. So decisions must be made. And they must be made amongst alternatives which have equal reason. So someone, an authority, in this case the conductor, has to determine how the music will be played. And the musicians must accept the conductor's determinations and play as she directs, or else there will be no music.

Does a musician lose his freedom when he plays as his conductor directs? He does lose his ability to play in any which way he might choose, but is that a loss of freedom? True, a trombonist might play any number of solos without recognizing an authority outside himself. And he might play those solos very well. And we might even pay money to go hear him. But even the best trombonist in the world cannot play Beethoven's *Eroica* symphony by himself. Without the authority of a conductor, that symphony never could be heard. By acknowledging her, the conductor's, authority, a greater expression of freedom is possible. There is more music that the trombonist is now free to play.

One can see that the more complex the musical ensemble, the more the need for authority. I have mentioned a soloist. There can be duets where each person seems to take her cue from the other, and the authority to lead, to initiate, slides back and forth intimately, gently, as in a romantic dance. There can be quartets where matters of interpretation are hashed out at length through the hours spent in preparation together; in such a case, the authority is shared democratically amongst all the members. Complex multi-movement symphonies require greater coordination and set forth exponentially greater possibilities of legitimate interpretation. Even the conductor finds herself under higher authority, as there must be determinations about which music will be played on what dates through the season (and rare is the conductor who can declare such matters by fiat).

It is the complexities of social organization, with their attendant localizations and focusings of authority, that make possible large-scale coordinated actions of human creativity. Think back to our trombonist. He is happy to work with his conductor, for he knows her from experience to be a sensitive interpreter of the music they perform. He would not always take things at the same tempo she does, but all things considered she is an admirable conductor. She has authority, and he acknowledges that she has it. One can imagine a conductor who lost her authority. There are bad judgments in music, and a pattern of them would lead to dissension among the players. She would lose authority if she failed to maintain the good of quality performance intelligently interpreted. Or alternatively, perhaps through the selection of music that never used trombones except in trivial spots, the trombonist might start to wonder if she really had his good in mind. She could lose authority this way too, by not intending the good of the musicians.

Thus, in a symphony, authority enhances what the musicians are capable of doing freely by promoting their good as distinct musicians and by making it possible for them to participate in the complex good of music played together. This example points to how the work of authority has to do not primarily with human inadequacies (immaturity and sin) but with human excellences. We see that true authority is exercised within reasonable bounds, yet makes determinations that go beyond what is given by reason. (A conductor can choose a wrong musical interpretation, yet there is not one single right interpretation.) Above all, our example shows that authority enhances the freedom to participate in corporate action, as it also enhances freedom for individual fulfillment within corporate action.

A Description of Authority

We have called the conductor an authority. But what do we mean by that word?

In English, the word has an obvious root: "author." We should understand this authorship as at once active and passive. An authority, who is able to "authorize" the actions of others, is at the same time one whose own actions are authorized. So does etymology place us at once within a world of interconnections. Authorities are not lone rangers or loose cannons; they are not disconnected and unaccountable. To be an authority is to be authorized by someone or something beyond oneself. Thus the centurion who had appealed to Jesus to heal his servant asked Jesus not to come to his house: "only speak the word, and my servant will be healed." This itself is an expression of faith in Jesus, that he is able to heal at a distance, simply by speaking. But the centurion's insight goes further. "I also am a man under authority," he says, "with soldiers under me; and I say to one, 'Go,' and he goes, and to another, 'Come,' and he comes." The centurion *has* authority because he is *under* authority. It is striking that he doesn't say to Jesus, "You and I are both authorities in our various realms; I am able to command and others do what I say; you too can command spirits and elements and they do what you say." Rather, he says first, "I also am a man under authority." His faith is that he sees Jesus as "a man under authority," implicitly, the authority of his Father.[1]

The Greek is *exousia.* Is it fanciful to see embedded here the word for "being," *ousia,* and thus a rooting of authority in our nature? Authority, *exousia,* is formed from *exesti,* a verb that exists only in the impersonal third person and has for its earliest meaning "it is allowed, it is in one's power, is possible."[2] And *exousia* in ordinary Greek meant the "ability to perform an action," early extended to a right of action or a right to

1 Mt. 8.5–10; cf. Lk. 7.2–9; direct quotations from NRSV.

2 *An Intermediate Greek-English Lexicon* (Oxford: Clarendon Press, 1889), s.v. "ἔξεστι."

disposal, particularly as that right was given from above. Nonetheless, we can note that this word that comes to mean power in the sense of authority is compounded from *ek* and *ousia*. That etymology gives us "out of being" or "from being," suggesting for the philosophical mind that human authority comes out of human being, that it is deeply in accord with our being as humans that we have authority.

The word becomes important in the Christian Scriptures. Gerhard Kittel, in his masterful *Theological Dictionary of the New Testament*, writes that *exousia* "is the power displayed in the fact that a command is obeyed." From the beginning, authority is related to obedience; authority is not coercive (for the obedience extracted under, for example, torture is hardly true obedience), yet neither is authority constituted by obedience. We might picture authority as a "downward" governance that is "displayed," but not caused, by an "upward" obedience. According to Kittel's study, in the New Testament *exousia* is "the power which decides" but which functions only "in a legally ordered whole" as a power given ultimately by God. Authority is a species of power, namely, a decisive power; nonetheless, the power of authority is never isolated from a divinely authorizing context. Kittel also emphasizes that *exousia* is active, a performative concept, "operative in ordered relationships" and "cannot be separated from its continuous exercise." In the Christian community it "denote[s] the freedom" that comes from the community's divine authorization. But strictly speaking the word means "the absolute possibility of action which is proper to God." God's authority, his "absolute possibility of action," can be seen in many places, including nature and, interestingly, even in God's tolerance of Satan's rule, "the power of evil... [that is] yet encompassed by the divine overruling." Christ has divine *exousia*, his "divinely given power and authority to act," which is identical with his own freedom, his "own rule in free agreement with the Father." And *exousia* is given to the Church as its authority and freedom as the community given "existence and nature [by] Christ."[3]

What is impressive is the cosmic unity that runs throughout this New Testament concept of authority. All authority comes from God and no thing, no being, no realm is outside his dominion. God's authority bestows power and freedom and is found preeminently in Christ and, after Christ, in the community that is in him.

3 Gerhard Kittel, *Theological Dictionary of the New Testament*, trans. Geoffrey W. Bromiley (Grand Rapids, Mich.: Eerdmans, 1964–76), s.v. "ἐξουσία," 2.562ff.

Thus the Christian Scriptures give theological depth to our prior intuitions, sparked by the English and Greek etymologies: that authority has to do with a web of authorizations, and that *that* has to do with the power or capacity to achieve fullness as a human being. In light of all this, I will now venture a working description of authority, to lay out in a rough way its boundaries.

Authority, I say, is held by a person or persons who lead humans to a fuller exercise of their freedom to accomplish human tasks. Such an authority will customarily appeal to other "authorities," including texts and other things and persons acknowledged to promote the human good—although it is only persons who can be authorities in the true sense. An authority is someone who is authorized (which is to say, an authority is also under authority). Conversely, to exercise authority is to be acknowledged as one who has authority (which is to say, normally, an authority is one who is able to summon free obedience). The fundamental attitude toward an authority is trust, yet at the same time one must acknowledge that authorities may be mistaken. This trusting attitude toward an authority persists even when one is in the very midst of arguing against an authority that one believes is mistaken. Reason is among the "authorities" that authority points to, but authority is itself something more than reason. It is a capacity to get things done, a determination and an ordering of what shall be done, and thus a particular species of power taken broadly. Yet authority is not, essentially, the power of coercive force. When coercion becomes necessary, authority is not able to be all that it could be.

The previous paragraph, I believe, identifies the features of authority to which we must attend if we are to understand it.

Social Authority

As we come to see the positive connections of authority and freedom we are at the same time coming to understand what it means to say that human beings have a social nature. Aristotle defined man as a "political animal," by which he did not mean that the exemplary human is a fraternity brother who eats, sleeps, and drinks in the details of government policy 24/7 (think, perhaps, the young policy wonk who later became President Bill Clinton). No, Aristotle meant simply that man is the animal who lives socially, in cities. (*Polis,* from which we get our word "political," is Greek for "city.") We live together, we humans. Show me a man alone, said Aristotle, and I say to you he is not a man: he is either a beast or a god.[4] Beasts can live in essential isolation, and yes one can imagine a person living alone in the woods and subsisting entirely on berries he picks and game he has caught. He is fully in touch with his physicality. But is he really a man? Even the great hermits of the early Christian centuries were social—entertaining visitors, dispensing advice, and teaching others how to be hermits.[5] On the other hand, a man alone might in some way have transcended his finitude and earthliness, and achieved a "spiritual" state that was godlike, indifferent, for instance, to the ravages and chances of time. He is indifferent to his body, to space and change, to history. Is he really a man?

Why are beasts and gods not human? What is it that makes human beings essentially social? It is our use of language. Words tie us together, creating shared memories, allowing us to entertain alternative possibilities, and providing the tools for cooperative action that goes beyond instinct. This is different than the cooperative behavior we see in other animals; they work together in the present, and their communications, lacking tense and mood, are not capable of presenting alternative reality. Animals can be brutal, but they lack the imagination for evil that allows humans to create systems of extermination. Animals can be good, but they lack the ability to imagine and bring about glorious cultural artifacts like universities, the microchip, the *Iliad*, and anesthetic dental surgery. And the gods? Aristotle, apparently, never asked the radical creation question; for that insight we have the Hebrews to thank. But once the radical creation question has been broached we realize (see Chapter 1 above) that the creator can in no way be thought of as a being inhabiting the universe. There cannot be two creators: not only for the reason that one would have had to create the other, but more profoundly (and paradoxically) because the notion of number applies only to beings that exist in the universe. I can have two cats (although I'd rather not, thank you); I'd call them two "cats" because there is such a thing as cat-nature and here before me would be two instances of it. But the distinction of nature and individual-with-the-nature does not apply to God. God is not an individual; *that's* why there can't be two of him. For God, "to be" and "to be God" are one and the same. (Which is also why God must exist, but there is nothing necessary about Victor Austin existing.)

We talk; we are social beings by our very nature. This means that to flourish as human beings, to be what we are, we need others. In the

4 See Aristotle, *Politics*, 1253a.

5 I am grateful to Stephen Hildebrand for this point.

case of a symphony orchestra, we saw that its member musicians could not flourish as musicians, could not be the musicians that they were, without the ordered society of the orchestra. And within that ordered society, authority is needed. The members are free to be the musicians they are (which is, of course, an active thing; they are free to perform and fulfill their musician-ness) in direct proportion to the presence of authority in the symphony.

The person who fully made this argument in the twentieth century was the French philosopher Yves Simon (1903–61).[6] After settling in the United States in 1938, Simon taught at Notre Dame and later was a member of the Committee on Social Thought at the University of Chicago. His corpus includes three significant works on authority: the 1940 Aquinas Lecture at Marquette, entitled *Nature and Functions of Authority*;[7] his most famous book, the 1951 *Philosophy of Democratic Government*;[8] and his posthumous 1962 volume, *A General Theory of Authority*.[9] While Simon argued that authority is necessary in practically every human endeavor, in what follows I confine myself to his analysis of the functions of authority in society.[10]

Simon agrees, uncontroversially, with what he calls "anti-authoritarian theorists" to this extent: that authority does have a proper function to play in situations of deficiency.[11] As we have seen already, there is a place for authority in the rearing of children, and likewise for those who suffer some other lack which makes it impossible for them to function as fully rational human beings. Yet such situations of deficiency,

6 For a short, competent, intellectual biographical overview, which gives an account also of the posthumous publications and influence of Simon, see Anthony O. Simon, "Editor's Note," in *idem*, ed., *Acquaintance with the Absolute: The Philosophy of Yves R. Simon* (New York: Fordham University Press, 1998). The same volume contains a "definitive bibliography" of Simon's works published both during his life and posthumously, from 1923 through 1996.

7 Yves Simon, *Nature and Functions of Authority* (Milwaukee: Marquette University Press, 1940; repr. 1948).

8 Yves Simon, *Philosophy of Democratic Government* (Chicago: University of Chicago Press, 1951; rev. ed. Notre Dame: University of Notre Dame Press, 1993). The 1993 edition is identical with the earlier, apart from an expanded index.

9 Yves Simon, *A General Theory of Authority* (Notre Dame: University of Notre Dame Press, 1962; repr. 1980 with new introduction by Vukan Kuic).

10 Simon sees a need for authority in social life, in seeking truth, and in what he calls the communication of excellence. "The communication of excellence" is, roughly, growth in virtue. With regard to seeking truth, Simon limits authority's role to one merely substitutionary, as I note in Chapter 3.

11 Simon, *A General Theory of Authority*, 21. Here and after I cite from the 1980 reprint.

Simon argues, cannot exhaust the role of authority in a society that is more than a contractual arrangement or partnership.[12] Simon admits that in a partnership, "the need for authority is never felt," except in "abnormal" situations, for the reason that a partnership is merely a coincidence of individual purposes.[13] If there is no disturbance, partners can each pursue their own interests without needing any authority. By contrast, a community, which involves common action and not merely the coincidence of individual purposes, needs some means to unify and bring about its common action. Here, so Simon argues, is the need for authority, and it is a necessity that has nothing to do with any deficiencies. But why does a community need authority in order to secure its common action?

The case rests on a correct understanding of human freedom.[14] One might think that to be free means that one's possible actions are undetermined; there is determination, and its opposite is freedom. But Simon sees freedom as an increase in human capacity. A free person can do more, not less, than an unfree person. His word for this state of freedom is "superdetermination," by which he means such a person is "determined" with respect to a number of things which he is able to do, and will have to choose which of them he will in fact bring about. Since Simon calls free choice "superdetermination," he understands freedom, not determinism, to be the opposite of "indetermination."[15]

12 "Authority thus does not, as such, arise out of sin or a lack or deficiency of some sort, though it may be called in to meet these situations also." James V. Schall, "Introduction: Immanent in the Souls of Men," in *Acquaintance with the Absolute*, 1–16, here 5.

13 *A General Theory of Authority*, 30–1.

14 Hannah Arendt famously is credited with saying that we fail to understand authority because we fail to understand freedom. See, for example, Robert N. Bellah, "Freedom, Coercion, and Authority," *Academe*, January/February, 1999, FindArticles.com, October 11, 2007 (http://findarticles.com/p/articles/mi_qa3860/is_199901/ai_n8845269): "Missing in the polarity between freedom and coercion is the concept of authority, which liberals tend to equate with coercion, but which an older tradition of political philosophy saw as the condition of freedom, not its antithesis. Indeed, following Arendt and Elshtain, one could argue that when authority disappears, freedom collapses into coercion."

15 See Vukan Kuic, "Yves R. Simon on Liberty and Authority," in *Acquaintance with the Absolute*, 128–46. See also the articles by Catherine Green, "Freedom and Determination: An Examination of Yves R. Simon's Ontology of Freedom," and S. Iniobong Udiodem, "Metaphysical Foundations of Freedom in the Social and Political Thought of Yves R. Simon," in *Freedom in the Modern World: Jacques Maritain, Yves R. Simon, Mortimer J. Adler*, ed. Michael D. Torre (Mishawaka, Ind.: American Maritain Association, 1989), 89–99 and 101–7 respectively.

What are the implications of this view that, the freer I am, the more there is that I am capable of doing? It means that when freedom increases, so do "causality and intelligibility." If there is more freedom, then there is more that can be *done* and more that can be *known* or understood by reason. Superdetermination, then, is characteristic of "extraordinary plenitude of being."[16] Simon writes:

> Few thinkers ever awoke to the theory that freedom is superdetermination rather than indetermination, and that its principle is more highly and more certainly *formed* than that of determinate causality; freedom proceeds, not from any weakness, any imperfection, any feature of potentiality on the part of the agent but, on the contrary, from a particular excellence in power, from a plenitude of being and an abundance of determination, from an ability to achieve mastery over diverse possibilities, from a strength of constitution which makes it possible to attain one's end in a variety of ways.[17]

As societies increase in complexity, we may think of them as increasingly formed in the sense that there is more that their members are capable of doing and comprehending. Simon adduces the further consideration that the objects of knowledge need not be, all of them, characterized by determinate relations. Increase of knowledge, then, may lead to an increase in the possibilities of human flourishing. That is to say, increase of knowledge need not result in narrowing of possible action.[18] It is not always the case that as we grow in knowledge our choices for flourishing become more limited. On the contrary, knowledge is "amplitude" of being: one knows more, can do more, is more free, is more human. "Knowledge, as we have said, is amplitude, and the more perfect it is, the greater source of abundance it becomes."[19]

16 *A General Theory of Authority*, 43.

17 Yves R. Simon, *Freedom of Choice* (New York: Fordham University Press, 1969), 152f. (This passage is translated from a philosophical encyclopedia that Simon was working on at the time of his death, appended as a summary to a book that is largely a translation of Simon's 1951 book, *Traité de libre arbitre*.)

18 *A General Theory of Authority*, 42. Philip Turner, in his highly perceptive dissertation, may under-emphasize this epistemological claim in his critique of Simon. See Philip Williams Turner III, "Theological Anthropology and the State: A Study of the Political Ethics of Yves Simon and Helmut Thielicke" (Ph.D. diss., Princeton University, 1978), esp. 178–85 and 192. I would like to add that I am grateful to Turner for first drawing my attention to Simon when I was a student and he the ethics professor at the General Theological Seminary.

19 Yves Simon, *An Introduction to the Metaphysics of Knowledge*, trans. Vukan Kuic and Richard J. Thompson (New York: Fordham University Press, 1990), 22. This book is a translation of *Introduction à l'ontologie du connaître* (Paris: Desclée de Brouwer, 1934).

Let's think about what this means for our orchestra. The stronger and more capable its members, the greater the range, the "abundance," that their repertoire can have. And simultaneously, a more capable orchestra is able to play any given repertoire in a more excellent way, with greater "amplitude." As an orchestra improves, it can play better and it can play more. This improvement is in both knowledge and power, and it does not narrow the possible performances of the orchestra. To the contrary, the better the orchestra, the more it will need something besides its own knowledge and power to make the necessary determinations of what will be played, when, how, and so forth.

This is why authority is necessary to a society. For if growth in virtue and excellence, in potency and knowledge, does not result in a limiting of our choices but instead effectively multiplies them, then reason and good will alone will be inadequate to make necessary determinations among the multiple possibilities for human flourishing. Those determinations, therefore, will have to be made by authority. This is authority's essential function. According to Simon, if it is to flourish a society needs to have steady action in pursuit of the common good. But if there are "a plurality of genuine means" that may be used for that common good, then unanimity based upon reason and good will cannot be "a *sufficient* method of steadily procuring unity of action."[20] Hence there must be authority, "*[t]he power in charge of unifying common action through rules binding for all.*"[21]

We should note that this conclusion is not an argument for any particular form of authority. For instance, the authority that society needs does not have to be a distinct body from the society itself. That is to say, the question of the *form* that authority should take is a separate question from the *necessity* of authority. Simon writes: "The problem of the need for authority and the problem of the need for a distinct governing personnel have often been confused."[22] Indeed, authority might take the form of a majority vote amongst all, and in a society without deficiencies, we would not need to worry about individuals then refusing their accession to the "rules binding for all" that authority provides. That is to say, Simon's account of this essential function defends authority without taking a position on any particular form of authority.

20 *A General Theory of Authority*, 47.

21 Ibid., 48.

22 Ibid., 49.

Once we see the necessary function of authority, a new question arises. If authority can issue binding rules for the attainment of a human good, is there not a danger of the suppression of the free agency of the members of society? Simon has considered this question, which takes us yet further to his deepest analysis.

When Simon considers the actual rich diversity characteristic of a free society, he makes a distinction between the "form" and "matter" of the common good. The "form" of the common good is, roughly speaking, the idea of the common good, while the "matter" points to the actual particular character of the common good in a given society at a given time. Simon argues that a society needs each person in it to will the form of the common good. If you don't do that, you are turning yourself against the attainment of the human goods that the society makes possible. Nonetheless, it is not necessary, *and would in fact be harmful to the society*, if each person also willed the particular matter of the common good. For if every person willed the matter of the common good, then society would become flat and dull, lacking the multitude of goods that its various members will to bring about.

Simon uses several examples to clarify this distinction of everyone willing the common good formally, on the one hand, from everyone not willing the common good materially, on the other. One of his examples involves parents with children who live along a dirt road. The common good of the community—so it is postulated—requires that the road be paved, yet the increased traffic would impose an increased risk to the safety of these parents' children. The parents should will the common good formally, that is, they should accede to the common good and be willing to abide by, and not obstruct, whatever determinations authority may make regarding the means to the common good. But, unless they are actually the authority itself or constituents of it (as could be imagined in a case of direct democracy), they are not obliged to will the matter of the common good—for instance, by getting the road paved on their own initiative, prior to and apart from any authoritative determination.[23]

23 See *A General Theory of Authority*, 58–9. Marianne Mahoney gives an exposition of how formally willing the common good while materially willing a particular good serves what she calls "Simon's insistence on the 'automatic goodness of the particular good'" in her essay, "Prudence as the Cornerstone of the Contemporary Thomistic Philosophy of Freedom," in *Freedom in the Modern World*, ed. Torre, 117–29.

Simon points to the fact that it would be harmful to society if particular goods were not materially willed precisely as particulars. The Latinist who refuses formally to will the common good will be an obstructive, harmful element of the faculty; but a faculty with no one passionately committed to Latin (i.e., materially willing the particular good of Latin studies) is an impoverished faculty.[24] When authority carries out its essential function of willing the matter of the common good, space is opened up for a freer and richer society in which the matter of particular goods is willed by particular agents, who nonetheless continue formally to will the common good. As Vukan Kuic observes, "contrary to superficial appearances, the common good of society rather than harmed is well served by individuals consciously and strongly dedicated to the promotion of particular goods."[25]

For Simon's point is also that each of society's ultimate units, each individual person, is a "totality" that is as magnificent as the universe as a whole. This totality that belongs to persons has a "unique character" that is not found in any social whole. It entails adherence to the good and mastery over one's own acts, that freedom and amplitude of being that Simon has stressed all along. Thus each member of a society "is all things; a family is a whole made of universes.... [A] family, a township, a county are particular subjects...but of these parts *the ultimate components are wholes which in a way comprehend all things.* At all levels of human association the presence of the person causes the energies of totality and liberty to be present."[26] Persons, therefore, are always more than their functions. That is to say, it is for the sake of persons, and not only for the sake of the common good of society, that persons must will particular goods, and not the common good, materially. Here we could speak of autonomy—Simon calls it an "excellence of autonomy"—which is fully in accord with the common good. The autonomy of each person, since he is a totality who encompasses the whole, cannot be a rebellion, but is rather the presence of an interiorized law, a condition "achieved through arduous progress." Autonomy thus understood "vindicates the particularity of the subject and whatever forms of authority are needed for the preservation of

24 See *Philosophy of Democratic Government*, 44–7. I cite from the 1993 edition.

25 Vukan Kuic, *Yves R. Simon: Real Democracy* (Lanham, Md.: Rowman & Littlefield, 1999), 63–9; here, 66.

26 *A General Theory of Authority*, 73; emphasis added.

this particularity."[27] Thus in Simon's deepest analysis, authority exists in order that human persons may flourish as self-governed members of society who somehow contain their society (societies) in themselves. The achievement of authority is for society to be taken into the individual, not vice versa.

Is Simon's argument persuasive? I will test it by raising three significant objections to this argument for the necessary functions of authority in society.

Objection 1. Why should we assume that reason does not uniquely determine our choices? Given the good we wish to pursue, and given people who are intelligent and of good will who wish to pursue the good, why would they not be able to ascertain the uniquely best way to pursue the good they desire? If there never are two or more equally reasonable ways to bring about a good, authority will not be essential, that is, will not be fundamentally necessary. At best, it could be helpful or prudent, but it would fall short of being necessary.

Objection 2. Why must we grant that there is a problem of everyone in a society willing the common good at once both materially and formally? It would seem that we can imagine our hypothetical Latinist arguing passionately for the inclusion of Latin in the curriculum while at the same time considering and weighing and understanding the arguments for proportion and balance in the curriculum as a whole.

Objection 3. Is this conception of authority dependent upon a model that, being structured, is implicitly "top-down"? Why are we thinking that we need to come to determinations of the means to achieve the common good, and that we need to have an agency that wills the common good materially? Determinations of how to achieve the common good need not be formalized; people from below can spontaneously organize themselves and, in fact, may do so better without the burden of authority watching over them.

These objections, it seems to me, are significant but not unanswerable.

Reply to objection 1. The first objection relies basically on a faith in reason's power to make unique determinations of what is best to do in any situation whatsoever. To this claim there is a straightforward epistemological rejoinder: how could we know? Even the weaker claim that, for most if not all of the time, reason will yield a unique determination

27 Ibid., 79. For a discussion of the subtleties in Simon's treatment of the common good, see Kuic, *Yves R. Simon: Real Democracy*, 52–8.

of the best means to achieve the common good—this weaker claim is based on an unproven, and unprovable, trust in reason's power. Of course, we should encourage responsible deliberation. But if a consensus is not reached today, do we carry the matter over until tomorrow? The objection would require that we do so, not only today but always, for it is premised on the notion that given enough time the uniquely best way to proceed will be discovered by reason. One might wonder if this objection fails to account for human finitude. Human beings of good will and intellectual maturity are still human beings, finite, situated in time and place and history. The argument is about the connection of *human* authority and *human* freedom; it is not about angels. And if we are right to think that an increase in knowledge brings about an increase in potency, then the longer deliberation continues, the more varied and complex the possibilities for action will become. The time required for deliberation could increase exponentially!

Reply to objection 2. To the second objection we might also profitably remember our finitude. Human beings can always do more to expand their imaginations, to take into account other perspectives, other histories, other goods. But we can never achieve a viewpoint-free understanding of the entire universe in a single all-encompassing vision. It is because we can never reach a "God's-eye view" that we need each other. Specifically, we need each other willing materially the particular goods that we see and know and care about. This is why we already know what it means for the Latinist to be passionate and reasonable: it is for him to argue for the goods of Latin study in *our* school at *this* time while acceding to the determinations of the curricular authorities, once made.

Reply to objection 3. The third objection seems to postulate an antithesis of freedom and authority. But we have seen reasons to hold that true authority enables and increases freedom, including especially the ability of persons to act in concert for goods that can be achieved only by corporate action. Nonetheless, there is no necessity for every decision to be made by a "top" authority. What might a non-top-down authoritative action look like? One violinist may help another without being told to do so: when such freely-offered assistance is accepted, authority is recognized. Or after a period of intense and difficult rehearsal, a percussionist may offer to buy everyone a drink, seeing that as a way of strengthening, in effect, the formal commitment each musician has to their common good. The objection rests, in other words, on a failure fully to grasp that authority and freedom are positively correlated. Furthermore, the requirement that individuals need to will the common good formally, while continuing to will more particular goods materially, means that no "top" authority is mandating with specific detail *how* those particular goods are to be pursued. Authority fosters a rich texture in society, not a flattening of initiative and purpose. In this way too authority is positively correlated with freedom, increasing the freedom of all.

Let me summarize what we have learned from Simon. Because freedom results in the multiplication of what is possible in action and what is conceivable in thought, authority has an essential function in making determinations concerning the multiplicity of means by which the common good of a society might be achieved. And because the common good of a society is not one isolated goal, but rather encompasses within itself the harmonious pursuit by many persons of a multiplicity of particular goods, the most essential function of authority is to will the matter of the common good, so that the various agents and associations within society can will the matter of particular goods. As Simon puts it, "authority is needed because it is desirable that particular goods should be taken care of by particular agencies."[28] If all persons of mature talents and good will were to turn their attention to the matter of the common good, the many non-common, particular goods of society would suffer and society would be, overall, less rich, less varied, less advanced.

Social authority, we have seen, rests on a right understanding of freedom. And we have seen Simon argue for the notion of freedom as superdetermination. Let us look more closely at the paradoxes of freedom and free action.

The Paradoxes of Freedom and of Free Action

Consider a detail, buried in Aquinas's reply to an objection to a question on fasting in the *secunda secundae* of his *Summa theologiae.* The question is whether the church did the right thing when it required of its members the keeping of certain fasts. Aquinas's answer is that fasting is a useful practice as an atonement for sin, a preventative for further sin, and a raising of the mind to spiritual things. He has also said that, on account of these reasons for fasting, our reason makes clear that we ought to fast. But reason alone would not specify certain times, nor would the manner of fasting be established by reason. To the church,

28 *A General Theory of Authority*, 72.

therefore, for the good of Christian people, lies the prescription of the times and manner of fasting.

Now the objector had dredged up a passage from Augustine to argue that the purpose of the Christian gospel as a whole had been to draw forth a free people. This people, Christian and free, should not be subject to a large number of regulations; in fact, a small number of sacraments was the entire extent of what was needed. Anything beyond these minimal sacraments would impinge Christian liberty, weighing the people down with "slavish burdens." Aquinas replies that the objector misunderstands Augustine but, more fundamentally, misunderstands freedom. Prescribed fasts, Aquinas writes, are not opposed "to the freedom of the faithful, rather are they of use in hindering the slavery of sin, which is opposed to spiritual freedom." In short, the determinations of authority were necessary because reason alone could not specify when and how to fast. And these determinations did not limit freedom, because, on the contrary, the fasting they called for would help set Christian people free from sin's bondage.[29]

This concept of freedom is paradoxical all the way down, as we can see in an earlier passage from the *Summa*. As he considered the New Law, which is the Gospel, Aquinas asked whether it ought to have any prescriptions or proscriptions at all. Are there *any* external acts that the Gospel ought to require or, conversely, forbid? The question of freedom is fundamental here: because the Gospel, which is the good news of liberation in Christ, should not bring about a new sort of slavery to external acts. Aquinas was considering a view that is held by many people today, that what matters is not what you do or don't do, but what is in your heart. To this, the gist of Aquinas's answer is that the New Law should and does prescribe those things that are necessary to salvation, and that it should and does proscribe those things that prevent salvation. But his analysis is subtle, as we shall see.

The objection is raised that the New Law should neither prescribe nor prohibit any specific external acts. And the reason is that the New Law is "the law of the Spirit," and "where the Spirit of the Lord is, there is liberty." But "there is no liberty when man is bound to do or avoid

29 Thomas Aquinas, *Summa theologiae* II-II, q. 147, a. 3, ad 3. Translation quoted is from the Fathers of the English Dominican Province, 2nd ed. (1920), as found on the Internet: http://www.newadvent.org/summa/. I am grateful to Jeremy Wilkins for drawing my attention to this passage.

certain external acts." Thus the New Law cannot require or proscribe them.[30]

Aquinas's reply to this objection is multi-layered. He quotes Aristotle to support the understanding of acting freely as to act of one's own accord. But a human being will act of his own accord only when he acts according to his nature; true human habits, that is to say, are inclinations in accord with nature. Aquinas has already established that the Holy Spirit gives us grace which is "like an interior habit" and thus inclines us to act rightly. Thus this grace "*makes us do freely* those things that are in keeping with grace, and shun what is opposed to it." So in addition to the sense that the New Law liberates us by requiring us to do or avoid those things we must in order to be saved, it is also the law of liberty because it "*makes us comply freely*" with such precepts and prohibitions. We comply freely because our actions are prompted by grace.[31]

But how can grace—the Holy Spirit—God—cause us to act freely? If I do something freely, don't I need to do it (as Aristotle said, and as Aquinas agreed) *of my own accord*? How can I do freely something that God causes me to do?

This is the deep paradox of freedom. It is a paradox, which means as I said in the first chapter that we are unable to grasp firmly or understand *how* it is. Nonetheless, it is possible to see why it is not a contradiction to say, of a particular action, both "I did that freely" and "God caused me to do that."

The reason is the peculiarity and singularity of God. God is the creative cause of everything that exists. Now to cause something to exist is not the same as to start it or to set it in motion. It is, rather, to give it being, to hold it in being. We can be misled here by the fact that we have two words, "create" and "sustain," which in truth apply equivalently to God's creative act. It is of course otherwise with human makings. If I make a chair, I am "creating" it in a sense (but not in a radical sense; I am using materials that already exist and just rearranging them into a chair). If I then neglect the chair I made, perhaps by putting it out where it is exposed to sun and rain and snow, and the chair then splinters to bits, you would rightly say I

30 *Summa theologiae* I-II, q. 108, a. 1, obj. 2. Translation quoted is from the Fathers of the English Dominican Province, rev. Daniel J. Sullivan, as reprinted in Robert Maynard Hutchins, ed., *Great Books of the Western World*, vol. 20, *Thomas Aquinas: II* (Chicago: Encyclopedia Britannica, 1952). The objector quotes Rom. 8.2 and 2 Cor. 3.17.

31 *Summa theologiae* I-II, q. 108, a. 1, ad 2; in both cases, emphasis added.

had failed to sustain the chair that I had made. For us, to make and to sustain are different. But when God makes the universe and all that is in it, he is not *starting* it, he is holding it in being, giving it its being every moment. Mortimer Adler had a word for this: he called it the *exnihilating* cause.[32] God is the cause of things not going out of existence.

This means, so at least Aquinas thought, that God would be capable of making a world without a beginning, a world with infinite past time.[33] And that might just be the kind of world we have, for we seem to be unable to know in principle what, if anything, existed prior to the Big Bang. There might have been an infinite number of previous universes, each of which re-collapsed into a singularity and then erupted with, well, a "bang" into its successor. Future scientific research may answer the question of whether the universe, or something, has always existed. Nonetheless, the point remains: whether we have a temporal beginning or not will make no difference to the claim that the universe is created. For to create is not the same as to begin.

Now God who creates—holds in being—everything that is, cannot himself be one of the things that he is holding in being. If God is going to be the creator, he can't create himself, because he himself can't be one of those things of whose being he is the cause. So, as I said more briefly in the first chapter's discussion of paradox, God is not a being in the universe; rather, he is the cause of everything's being. We could say, to emphasize God's strangeness, that God is not caused; God is not a being; God is no thing; that you cannot put God alongside anything else; that God's essence is his existence (God's nature is no different from his actuality); God is not an individual; God is a member of no species; there could never be another God.

One has to admit that these are odd things to say. Indeed, as Brian Davies puts it, God is himself very odd.[34] And so we should not be surprised that when we speak of God we must speak paradoxically. To return to freedom, I offer an example of what God's causality is *not* like. If I pointed a gun and told you to sign over to me all your real property, your signature would not be accepted as valid, on the

32 See, for example, Mortimer Adler, *How to Think About God* (New York: Macmillan, 1980), chapter 14.

33 In *Summa theologiae* I, q. 46, a. 2, Aquinas argues that it is an article of faith, and not a deliverance of reason, that the world has a beginning.

34 Brian Davies, *The Reality of God and the Problem of Evil* (London: Continuum, 2006), 78–80.

ground that it was not freely given. I caused you to do it; *therefore*, it was not something you did of your own. But if you, one bright day, found yourself contemplating what incomparable benefits you had derived from reading my illuminating book, and in gratitude you decided to send me, perhaps not a deed to your property, but a bottle of fine port, no one would say I ought to send it back. Everyone would say, you freely gave that port to Austin, and so it's his. And I would say, God caused you to give that port to me, freely.

Free actions are truly human actions, and God is just as much a cause of them as he is a cause of planets hurtling through empty space and enzymes dissecting my dinner into the stuff that makes blood cells and the stuff that clogs my arteries.[35] Again, our normal language deceives us. Your insurance may cover your car repair if someone bashes into it, while excluding, and thus not covering, the repair needed because a hurricane causes a dam to break. At least colloquially, the latter (but not the former) is called an "act of God." But normal language misleads us here. Everything that is, is caused by God. God causes gravity and inertia just as much as he causes your acts of generosity. In fact, Aquinas says, God is even more so the cause of the things we do freely than he is the cause of things that happen according to (as we put it) laws of nature.

That's because things that happen by nature are understandable on the purely natural level. Why is the kettle boiling? We can say: because the gas is causing it to boil. There is a natural explanation. We could also say, and it would be true, that God is causing the kettle to boil. But God is doing so by means of the gas. When we ask about free actions, that middle ground, the natural cause, is gone. That's precisely what we mean when we say that they are free. Why is Georgina boiling? Because she is responding to the injustice she has just witnessed of me pulling a gun on you. Georgina is acting freely, and is "super-determined" towards a number of things that she might do: shout at me, pull a gun of her own, call for help. But if, in a different circumstance, we were to say Georgina is boiling because 20 minutes ago she took too much of her medicine, then her boiling would have a natural cause and would not be a free action.

The important thing to note is the difference between saying "Austin caused you to do X" and "God caused you to do X." Because God is not a being in the universe, there is no contradiction between your

35 God, however, is not the cause of evil actions. See ibid., 183–90.

choosing to do something freely and our simultaneous understanding that God is causing you to make that free choice.

Might we then say that God is the *author* of our free actions? If they are truly free they will be in accord with our true nature as human beings, and so a free action is also a fulfilling action. Simon said that freedom is superdetermination: it is having many things to which we are determined and making choice amongst them. So, I think unquestionably, free actions are good things. Should we think of them in connection with the collect that addresses God as "the author and giver of all good things"? Narrative ethics has played with the analogy of authorship, urging us to think of ourselves not as individuals who must seek to do our duty or, alternatively, maximize good outcomes, but as characters in a story who should seek to act, freely, as God has authored us to be. Such considerations lead us from the fundamental paradoxes of freedom back to questions of freedom and authority.

God is indeed the authority who not only brings into being all that is but who, by authorizing others, creates the possibility for people to flourish as full human beings in societies. Our argument thus returns to the etymology of authority, and to Christian theology's recognition of a structure of authority that extends from the heights to the depths wherever there are free beings: "I also am under authority, and I say to one..." So to speak of authority is, at the end, simply to speak of God as creator of free actions, with our focus on actors who are free, the social animal who needs society in order to find fulfillment of his nature: a fulfillment that is active, participatory, and we can now say authorized.

Social Authority Comes in a Living Person

When, earlier in this chapter, I ventured a definition of authority, I said it is persons who hold authority. Such a claim runs contrary to our normal use, according to which many things are called authorities. In the Christian churches, for instance, Scripture is regarded as a, and sometimes the, supremely important authority. Traditions are often reckoned as authorities. Constitutions, laws, and precedents are called authorities. Where I live there is a vast and important, although impersonal, bureaucracy called the Metropolitan Transportation Authority. Books and other documents from the past are treated as authorities by practitioners in their field. So it would seem that authorities can be many things other than persons.

The method of medieval theology was to reconcile the authorities. We see this method at its best in Aquinas. Aquinas cites many authorities; he charmingly cites Aristotle as "the Philosopher" and Paul as "the Apostle," so important are they. Yet no authority in the sense of a written document—not even Aristotle, not even the Bible—is dispositive for a question at hand. The reason is that written authorities at least seem to say different things, and thus they have to be read with a rational mind. Reason, which deals with the authoritative sources and brings them to bear on a particular question, and interprets the authorities in order to make distinctions so as to reconcile what they say while answering the given question, thus becomes itself an authority. We can speak of this process of reconciling authorities as "the authority of reason."

Yet, I say, neither documents nor dead persons nor bureaucratic institutions nor even reason can be, in the true sense, an authority. If we think of Aquinas using his reason, reconciling the authoritative writings, and answering the thousands of questions that he did in his great *summae* and elsewhere, we realize that over the nearly 750 years since his death Aquinas's own writings became new authoritative writings that future students had to learn, on top of the authorities Aquinas himself had worked with. That is to say, while Aquinas used reason to reconcile the authorities he had, the result for us is that we have more "authorities," that is, more writings. We don't, from them or in them, have actual authority. *Without the living authority of a scholar actively engaged in the work that scholars do, which includes the study of "authoritative" texts, authority is at best latent or potential; it is not actual authority.* To make the point general: *without the living authority of persons doing what authorities do, there is no authority.*

Those of us who are Anglicans like to say that we have three sources of authority: Scripture, tradition, and reason. But what needs to be seen is that Scripture is just words on a page, reason but a name for an activity, and tradition just a ghost of an idea, until we have a person or persons, authorities, who are actively doing what authorities do.

It is the living Aquinas who is an authority, providing not just answers to questions but a model for how to do that. It is the symphony conductor, as we say, "at work" who is an authority. We must see this clearly: real authority is never present to us except as it is exercised by a person.

As an aside, this shows the wrong-headedness of arguments against "merely human authority." It is no mark against the Catholic Church that it has a pope (although, on the other hand, neither is it a mark for it). For every church, like every society of whatever sort, unless it is moribund, will have persons who have authority, who are in authority, who are, that is to say, authorities. There is no authority save that which comes to us in a human person.

Charisma: Follow Me and Find Yourself

The human good requires that there be authorities. This truth is rooted in the social aspect of our nature, that to be human is to be in society with other humans. But for a society to pursue its good, there must be determinations of the means to that good. Authority gives to society a particular concretization from amongst the many possibilities that are open to it (possibilities that only increase in number as a society becomes more complex). And by taking upon itself the material willing of the common good, authority frees the members of a society to will materially goods that are more particular, while those members grant their formal will to the common good.

In its best functioning, authority will be seen as intent upon the good of society's members, not only in themselves but also in larger contexts. A real authority will be seen as a person who acts "with authority," that is, as a person who is herself "under" authority. This means that a real authority is not seen as an individual isolated from a larger context. A real authority is not a lone person at the top of a pyramid of power. Rather, she is herself related to other mini-societies and other more encompassing societies. To be an authority is to be connected within the complex web of interrelationships that God has given so that humans may be free. An authority within a given society connects that society's good to the larger human good.

The correctness of the actual determinations of authority, lying as they sometimes must beyond the determinations of reason alone, may be opaque to particular members of the society. Nonetheless, a real authority will be trusted and granted the recognition that she does intend the good of the society at hand and of its members. That this recognition may be misplaced, that authority can make mistakes, err, and even become corrupt, is a topic to be taken up in Chapter 6. Here we focus on the place of authority in society in general, its necessary role, quite apart from questions of sin or immaturity, to provide the conditions for human beings to flourish as humans.

Authority is a performative concept. It needs to be continuously exercised. We speak of an authority (person) as "having" authority, but it is had only when it is in play. In the popular sense, an authority is someone who has charisma.[36] An authority is attractive, charismatic; she causes us to want to follow her. It's as if the conductor were to say, "Follow me, and you will discover what it really means to be a musician." Indeed, the implicit message of any authority is just that: "Follow me, and you will discover what it really means to be human."

Follow me, and you will find yourself. That is a decent paraphrase, I think, for the message of Jesus to his disciples: that they, by following him, would learn what it means to be human. Jesus, in Christian doctrine, is a full human being, indeed the sole human to be fully such, since all the rest of us are afflicted by sin, and since sin is essentially a subtraction from our true being. To follow Jesus is to follow the one who is truly human. But to be human is not to be alone: Jesus *needed* disciples, he needed to be in society if he was to live a fully human life. The disciples too, in following him, were promised that they would become "fishers of men," drawing to themselves human beings and thus forming new instances of the new society that is the church. Their authority comes from Jesus; in following a disciple, people would be recognizing that the disciple's authority connected them with the society that itself recognized Jesus' authority. And in following a disciple, people would be recognizing that the disciple, imitating Jesus in this, was an authority who intended their good: their free actions as human beings.

The charismatic element is not limited to religious authority. The coach, the conductor, the teacher, the foreman, the head nurse on the night watch: every authority which is truly such has an intangible, attractive quality, something beyond what reason can say and yet never contrary to reason, something which says, "Follow me, and you will find yourself and live freely as a real human being."

36 "Charisma," of course, is grace, and true charisma cannot be separated from morality, obedience, authority. Our culture's inability to understand authority is vividly pictured in the amoral (thus shallow and false) charisma of what is called "celebrity culture." On this, see Philip Rieff, *Charisma: The Gift of Grace, and How It Has Been Taken Away from Us* (New York: Pantheon Books, 2007).

Chapter 3

AUTHORITY AND TRUTH: EPISTEMIC AUTHORITY

Authority and Our Flourishing as Beings Who Know

By exploring the relation of freedom and authority, the last chapter showed how it is that we humans need authority simply in order to be what we are, because to be human is to live socially, and to live socially at all beyond the most minimal level requires authority. Too often thinking about authority jumps directly into political discussion and then finds itself at sea, drifting and confused, because it has failed first to get a hold on authority's social importance. Now at this point the reader might think that, the study of freedom and authority having been made in Chapter 2, it is time to move on to politics, to (what many think to be) the real heart of the matter. Yet to move thus from society to politics would be a naive trajectory of thought. Part of what this book intends to show is that politics is seriously important to our human fulfillment. But politics is neither the beginning nor the end of our discussion. Having seen that authority is rooted in our nature (recall the etymological clue: authority, as *exousia*, comes out of our being), the reader could intuit even at this early stage of the argument that authority may perdure beyond the grave, beyond the reach of any tax man, beyond the realm of earthly politics, all the way into redeemed human nature. Even as there is no authority-free human society, so it may be that there is no authority-free human future.

Yet however it turns out in the end that is on the far side of earthly politics, here I want to argue for the inclusion of a crucial earlier step, intermediate between society and politics. That step, for those who wish to understand authority, is the role authority plays in the apprehension of truth. Just as authority is essential to our flourishing as social beings, so (I say) authority is necessary if we are to flourish as beings who have knowledge. To see this will require that we dig into the paradoxes of the human grasp of truth, even as in the previous chapter we had to grapple with the paradoxes of human free action. This chapter will make a case that there is such a thing as epistemic authority. And like social authority, epistemic authority is necessary to us on two levels. First, it is exercised by persons to whom one must submit in the process of learning. So this chapter will speak of apprenticeship and trust. Yet one does not outgrow the need for authority, because (the second level) even a person who has epistemic authority is himself always subject to the judgment and review of others similarly situated with whom he is necessarily interrelated. Hence, on the first level, every knower is dependent upon authority in order to come to know. And on the higher level, every epistemic authority is also dependent upon (because interlocked with) the authority of others. All knowledge is interconnected.

Upon reflection, perhaps it is no surprise that epistemic authority so parallels social authority, and in that respect this chapter complements the analysis of social authority given previously. For truth and freedom are related. This is a theological claim as well as a philosophical: in St. John's Gospel, Jesus declares that it is the truth that sets us free. It is an anthropological claim: to succeed at being a human is both to be a social being and also to be a being who knows. Knowing is essentially connected to our sociality.

Yet none of this will be obvious if we think of knowing in common yet false ways. Allow me a crude sketch of a certain popular schizophrenia in knowledge. On the one hand, individuals, unconnected in any essential way with society or the world, are imagined to come to know something about the world that is "objectively" true. This is the view of knowledge as "facts" which are true apart from any human involvement. On the other hand, persons are supposed to believe things they want or have chosen to believe; according to this second view, there is no "objective" world but everything is "subjective" and thus "relative." Now many folks are quite capable of believing both these things at once, for instance—to take but one strategy among many—by means of an unreflective distinction of facts (objective, impersonal, unchanging) from values (subjective, personal, relative). Such a strategy manifestly has failed to answer important ethical issues—people divide, for instance, over whether the dignity of a human being is a fact or a value. The failure of such strategies should point to a need for reexamination.

We need to think of coming to know in a more subtle way. Let me ease into an analysis of epistemic authority by looking at one such authority in action.

Illustration: A Judge Deciding a Case

Consider a judge who has to reach a decision in a case before her. It is truth that she is looking for. As she ponders her decision, she is searching for the truth of the matter. She is trying to find out what the law says about this particular case. She wants the judgment to which she comes to be true judgment, that is to say, the truth about the matter at hand in the light of the law.

But how will she know what is the truth about the case? A person watching her from the outside would likely think there were a number of different ways she might decide. And from the outside, the choice between those varying outcomes could well appear arbitrary. To an outsider, it can seem that the judge will decide the way she *wants* to decide; that, various outcomes being conceivable, the determination between them will be made on extrinsic grounds. A person of a skeptical or cynical disposition might go so far as to say that whoever offers her a payoff, or whoever appeases her vanity the best—that's the way the case will go.

But such conclusions and speculations are possible entertainments only for outsiders. The subjective experience of a judge is quite different. She realizes, of course, the range of possible outcomes; indeed, given her understanding and experience, the range may be a good deal wider than the outsider or cynic can imagine. Yet what grips her interest is not the range of possibilities; it is the law. Her intelligence is not drawn outward to the variety of possibilities, but downward to the uniquely correct outcome of the case—the truth, which may be very hard to see. Where is the judge looking? She examines other judgments for apt parallels and correspondences to the case before her. She may consult with her peers for their insights as well. And she does this looking, weighing, and comparing by means of a body of practice that she brings with her—her experience, and also the experience of her entire profession as it has entered into her. By means of this body of practice she has the skill to identify appropriate parallel cases—precedent—while sifting out all that is irrelevant.

If we ask the judge what she is doing, she will say that she is trying to discover "the law in this case," to find out what the law *already says* about it. And that is a remarkable thing for her to say, because of course the law, being general, has not in fact spoken on this particular. The judge describes her situation as a matter of discovery, yet what she is looking for is so hidden it has never before been seen. She experiences within herself the lure to find something that is real and independent of her knowing and yet hidden.

So she proceeds. Driven by her intellectual passion to discover the truth, she hunts down the law in this case, and as she does so, the range of options before her narrows, until at the end her discretion evanesces. At that point the verdict of the law appears to her, and she pronounces judgment on the case, thereby committing herself to the truth of her judgment.

It is a commonplace to say the judge is an authority on the law. What we should note in this illustration of coming to a judgment is that her being an authority is what lays the ground for her being able to discover the truth. Outsiders, who lack her authority, are not so able to find the truth, and are thus more easily tempted to bypass the epistemological question and replace it with assertions of will or self-interest or raw power.

But when we attend to the subjective experience of the judge, we see how her experience is the same as that of any person who seeks the truth in whatever matter may be before him. It could be a research chemist trying to understand bacteria, or a mathematician trying to determine the truth of an equation, or a janitor trying to abate a persistent build-up of mold in the bathroom. Our own experience testifies that, when we seek to know something, we are seeking to know something that is somehow independent of us, particularly, independent of our asserting of its truth. Hence we cannot be faithful to our own experience of coming to the truth about a matter and, at the same time, hold that truth is solipsistic (I am the only truth I can know) or relativistic (what's true for me might not be for you). Nonetheless, the sole means for us to come to any truth is through our personal commitment. Thus, while we reject solipsism and relativity in truth, we also cannot maintain that truth is objective in the sense that it could be known impersonally or without passions or commitment. Now one might think that relativism and objectivity were alternatives that, between them, exhausted the field. But the illustration of the judge, and our own experiences of coming to knowledge, expose a more complex reality—more paradoxical—than those alternatives would suggest. In the middle ground which is our human reality of knowing, lying between both relativism and impersonal objectivity, we find authority.

That is what the judge is doing as she reaches her verdict. She is *personally committed* to finding *the truth about the matter.* And what she, a good judge, is looking for is not a reality that exists only inside her, or that is true only for her. She is looking for the truth of the matter. And she is able to find *it*, and not issue a verdict that is merely disguised self-assertion, because she exercises epistemic authority. She thus indicates to us that an indispensable function of authority resides in human knowing.

I say "indicates," because the judge has given us only an illustration of an argument, and not the argument itself. Let us now look more closely.

Epistemic Authority

Pilate famously asked Jesus, "What is truth?" Many people take Pilate's question to be a pseudo-question only, and for all I know they are right to do so. But Pilate is not right, if this is what he is doing, to reject the possibility of truth. Nor is it necessary, just because some people are skeptics, to say that, before we can speak of truth, we have to fend off the skeptical attack. For although there is skepticism, and although there are persons who reject the possibility of truth, it is nonetheless our common experience as human beings that we do have knowledge. We know that we know things, even if we do not know how this can be. In this book I am seeking insight into how things stand with us as humans: from our nature, to our governed life together, all the way to our ultimate destiny. So in bringing up the question of truth with respect to authority, I am asking roughly "how things are," as one might make some ordinary reference to "the truth of the matter."

When we think about the place of authority in our coming to know what's true, we might think that authority's place is limited to substitutionary functions.[1] Epistemic authority clearly does have substitutionary functions. A student needs to be guided by authorities until he comes to know—and then, it seems, he leaves the authorities behind.

1 For an instance of this view, see Richard T. De George, "The Nature and Function of Epistemic Authority," in R. Baine Harris, ed., *Authority: A Philosophical Analysis* (University, Ala.: University of Alabama Press, 1976), 76–93.

Or, because of the complexity of knowledge, no one can know more than a sliver of what is there to be known. Thus even experts need epistemic authorities to guide them in all fields except their own. But in either case—the student who is learning, or the expert who has mastered his field—authority is needed only when there is a lack of knowledge, and once knowledge is obtained—once truth is known—authority can be left behind.

Such in fact was the view of Yves Simon. Simon, who discerned so perceptibly the necessary functions of authority in society (as we saw in Chapter 2), thought that, in matters of theoretical cognition, the only functions of authority were substitutionary.[2] In Simon's analysis, epistemic authority differs in this regard from social authority because it has a different subject matter. Social authority has to do with practical judgment; it is concerned with the answer to the question "What shall we do?" As we have seen, even fully mature persons cannot dispense with authority (indeed, they need authority all the more) because of the expansive possibilities for coordinated action that are brought about by their freedom and excellence. By contrast, says Simon, theoretical cognition is concerned with objective truth, with the answer to the question, "What are the things?" And whenever authority must be invoked to address questions of truth, there has been a failure of intellect—that is, a failure truly to know. If I answer the question "What are the things?" by the assistance of authority, Simon states that to that extent I cannot be said truly to understand "the things."

Simon elaborates the difference between social and epistemic authority by means of the following contrast. In matters of action what we need is a leader, but to come to understand the truth what we need is a witness. Yet while we will always need a leader for our human social activity, we will not always need a witness for the truth. A witness, unlike a leader, has no power to give orders or to command obedience. A witness simply points: and if you then see what she, the witness, points to, you no longer need her. Underlying Simon's argument is the conviction that truth is objective. As he states, when someone comes to understand the truth, there is a "victory of objectivity [that] is the perfection of knowledge. *Under fully normal circumstances the determination of the theoretical assent involves neither authority nor liberty: it is an issue settled by objectivity alone.*"[3]

2 For the following discussion, see *A General Theory of Authority*, chapter 3, "The Search for Truth."

3 *A General Theory of Authority*, 87; emphasis original.

Simon's account of knowledge, as I have said, might well draw our initial assent. Yet there are questions that it would be appropriate to ask. We might ask—thinking again of our judge working towards her judgment of truth—whether it is right to understand knowledge as essentially objective. Objective knowledge would seem to lack any personal contribution from the knower: it is just out there, for the witness to point to. But is knowledge best thought of as impersonal? Is it truly free from dependence upon the knower? We might ask whether knowledge is independent of the passions of the knower, particularly the passion that is the desire to know—the intellectual passion that we saw cultivated and in play in the thinking of the judge. On the other hand, if we start to entertain the possibility that knowledge is not simply "objective," that it is "personal" and always is put forth with the conviction that it is true, have we moved away from "knowledge" itself and started on a descent into the quicksand of subjectivity?

Such questions suggest, it seems to me, that Simon's account of the relationship of authority and truth—indeed any account that presumes the impersonal objectivity of knowledge—is not adequate to our human knowing. Yet there are some suggestions in Simon's work that, had his life not been cut short, his thought could have developed along lines congenial to at least some of the points made below in this chapter.[4] With that as valedictory, I now turn to the scientist-cum-philosopher Michael Polanyi (1891–1976), whose great labor was to show, without falling into subjectivism or relativism, that true knowledge is ever personal.

Although his importance is in his refreshing examinations of what he called "personal knowledge," Polanyi began his professional career as a scientist, where his contributions within the field of chemistry were significant and included notable articles in professional publications over some four decades.[5] Then, prompted by political

4 For instance, that there is a silent "treasure" of established truth that is unspoken, because no longer questioned. However, in contrast to the argument I am about to make, Simon considers this silent truth to be essentially and fully speakable. See *A General Theory of Authority*, 89, which book, we should remember, was published posthumously. It strikes me as more than barely possible that Simon would have revised his views, had his life not been cut short and had he lived to read the mature epistemological works of Michael Polanyi. That he was not unaware of Polanyi we see in a footnote, *A General Theory of Authority*, 83 n. 3.

5 The bibliography of his work includes, besides Polanyi's 20 books, 218 scientific papers from 1910 to 1949, and goes on for another 14 pages with other articles, essays, reviews, and films. Harry Prosch, *Michael Polanyi: A Critical Exposition* (Albany: State University of New York Press, 1986), 319–46.

and philosophical concerns raised by the practice of science, such as the proper freedom of the scientist and, not incidentally (as we will see later) the problem of error, Polanyi redirected his distinguished intellectual career and took up investigations of the nature of knowledge. His turn to more philosophical writing was occasioned by his reflections on the need for scientific research to be free of externally imposed agendas. The relation of freedom and truth is at the heart of Polanyi's philosophy; he had grasped the human paradox that thought is compelled to pursue freely the truth.[6]

Polanyi's epistemology has received the sustained and ongoing attention of thinkers in many fields, including that of some esteemed theologians.[7] His epistemology is found in three major works. *Personal Knowledge: Towards a Post-Critical Philosophy*, which grew out of his 1951–52 Gifford lectures, bears its thesis in its title: all knowledge is personal, yet the personal character of knowledge does not make it any the less knowledge in truth.[8] It was followed in 1959 by *The Study of Man*[9] and then in 1966 by *The Tacit Dimension*.[10]

6 His reflections ultimately led him to his book in defense of intellectual liberty, which, he says, "is justified in general to the extent to which we believe in the power of thought and recognize our obligation to cultivate the things of the mind." This is not a defense of private individualism. Michael Polanyi, *The Logic of Liberty* (Chicago: University of Chicago Press, 1951); here v. For an account of Polanyi's intellectual journey, see Prosch, *Michael Polanyi*.

7 This despite Polanyi's rather slight considerations of Christian faith. Among the theologians who give credit to Polanyi's influence on their work are the scientist-theologian John Polkinghorne and the late systematic and fundamental theologian Avery Dulles. See Polkinghorne, *Science and Theology: An Introduction* (London: SPCK, 1998), esp. Polkinghorne's development of a position of "critical realism"; Polkinghorne, *The Faith of a Physicist* (Minneapolis: Fortress, 1996); Dulles, *The Craft of Theology: From Symbol to System*, expanded ed. (New York: Crossroad, 1995); Dulles, "Foreword," in Martin X. Moleski, *Personal Catholicism: The Theological Epistemologies of John Henry Newman and Michael Polanyi* (Washington, D.C.: Catholic University of America Press, 2000), ix–xiii. Here I would like to record my gratitude to Polkinghorne and Dulles who, independently of each other, introduced me to Polanyi when I was a graduate student at Fordham University.

For an account of the scholarly discussion on Polanyi's Christian faith (or lack thereof), see Moleski, *Personal Catholicism*, 58–60.

8 Michael Polanyi, *Personal Knowledge: Towards a Post-Critical Philosophy* (Chicago: University of Chicago Press, 1958). Hereinafter, all references to this book are to the corrected edition (Chicago: University of Chicago Press, 1962).

9 Michael Polanyi, *The Study of Man* (Chicago: University of Chicago Press, 1959).

10 Michael Polanyi, *The Tacit Dimension* (Garden City, N.Y.: Doubleday, 1966).

All knowledge is personal. In making this argument, Polanyi wages a relentless attack upon the "illusion" and "false ideal" that true knowledge is impersonal and detached—in a word, strictly objective: "complete objectivity as usually attributed to the exact sciences is a delusion and is in fact a false ideal."[11] Yet neither is knowledge merely subjective.[12] Polanyi painstakingly demonstrates that there is an "art" to knowing, and one needs to acquire the art in order to know.[13] There is never any knowledge that is independent of the knower.[14] And there is never a knower who is indifferent to her knowledge. We cannot get away from having and using intellectual passions and inarticulate commitments. These things are ever-present in us (and are not defects in knowledge; they are defects only on the supposition of the false ideal of objectivity).[15] Polanyi is well-known for his account of the "tacit dimension" that belongs to all knowledge. With regard to anything, what we know is always greater than what we are able to say.[16] By means of these fundamental claims Polanyi argues for an understanding of knowledge that is neither, on the one hand, impersonally objective, nor, on the other hand, solipsistic or relativistic.[17] These fundamental claims of Polanyi's are widely expounded, and I commend the footnotes to the reader who wishes to pursue their intricacies beyond the limited purposes I make of them in this chapter.[18]

The late patristics scholar Richard Norris found the opening of *The Study of Man* worth quoting at length for its concise exposition of a contradiction at the heart of the idea of objective, impersonal knowledge—namely, finding a place to stand.

11 *Personal Knowledge*, 18.

12 Ibid., chapters 8–10.

13 Ibid., chapters 1–4.

14 See *The Study of Man*, esp. chapter 1, which functions also as a reprise of the corresponding arguments of *Personal Knowledge*, and thus an introduction to them.

15 See *Personal Knowledge*, chapter 6; further developed in *The Tacit Dimension.*

16 *Personal Knowledge*, chapter 5.

17 "This position is not solipsistic, since it is based on a belief in an external reality and implies the existence of other persons who can likewise approach the same reality. Nor is it relativistic." *Personal Knowledge*, 316.

18 See, for example, Richard Gelwick, *The Way of Discovery: An Introduction to the Thought of Michael Polanyi* (New York: Oxford University Press, 1977); Jerry H. Gill, *The Tacit Mode: Michael Polanyi's Postmodern Philosophy* (Albany: State University of New York Press, 2000); Mark T. Mitchell, *Michael Polanyi* (Wilmington, Del.: ISI, 2006); Moleski, chapter 2; Prosch, esp. chapters 4–13; Drusilla Scott, *Everyman Revived: The Common Sense of Michael Polanyi* (Grand Rapids, Mich.: Eerdmans, 1995 [reprint of 1985 ed.]).

> Man's capacity to think is his most outstanding attribute. Whoever speaks of man will therefore have to speak at some stage of human knowledge. This is a troublesome prospect. For the task seems without end: as soon as we had completed one such study, our subject-matter would have been extended by this very achievement. We should now have to study the study that we had just completed, since it, too, would be a work of man....
>
> This difficulty may appear far-fetched, but it is, in fact, profoundly characteristic both of the nature of man and of the nature of human knowledge. Man must forever try to discover knowledge that will stand up by itself, objectively, but the moment he reflects on his own knowledge he catches himself red-handed in the act of upholding his knowledge.[19]

This is one of Polanyi's many commonsense illustrations of the reality, under-appreciated, that we always know more than we can say, for we not only know that which we assert, but we also (at one and the same time) uphold that knowledge with tacit understandings and skills which are not the focus of our awareness but are yet necessarily present in a subsidiary way.

Polanyi insists that we can come to knowledge only by means of the artful mastery of complex skills which never can be articulated or specified with exactitude. Learning involves acquiring a "connoisseurship" which "can be communicated only by example."[20] This applies even in the so-called hard or exact sciences, for practicing scientists must rely on their developed skills to distinguish relevant data from irrelevant. To take but a very simple example: a thermometer does not impersonally deliver the facts about temperature. Rather, it must be "read"; one learns how to interpret its markings, how to hold and care for the instrument, how to recognize a reading that must be false, how to calibrate the instrument and measure it against others. It is a skillful art to be able to know when a thermometer reading tells you the temperature, and when the reading tells you to throw away the thermometer. Polanyi observes that "[t]he large amount of time spent by students of chemistry, biology and medicine in their practical courses shows how greatly these sciences rely on the transmission of skills and connoisseurship from master to apprentice.... [T]he art of knowing has remained unspecifiable at the very heart of science."[21] Common conceptions of the objectivity of scientific knowledge will not hold up

19 *The Study of Man*, 11–12. Norris quotes this passage in his contribution to Geoffrey Wainwright, ed., *Keeping the Faith: Essays to Mark the Centenary of "Lux Mundi"* (Philadelphia: Fortress, 1988), 84.

20 *Personal Knowledge*, 54.

21 Ibid., 55.

under Polanyian scrutiny, for such knowledge is artfully acquired, in subtle ways that are unspecifiable in principle. A related point: researchers are committed—beyond any reason they could give—before they begin experiments to what the likely results are; they do not employ a false objectivity or agnosticism which takes every datum as equal and waits indifferently for the results to present themselves.[22]

What this complex of arguments says about authority is subtle. Personal knowledge requires the development of skills, and that development itself requires something that can rightly be called apprenticeship. And an apprentice is one who submits to authority. But note: what an authority conveys is knowledge that always includes, as part of what is known, tacit and unspeakable (in principle, not simply unspoken) components. In other words, Polanyi shows us that epistemic authority is essential, and not merely substitutionary, because knowledge is personal and not merely objective.

For one cannot acquire skills—become an adept or connoisseur in one's field—in isolation, say, through reading alone; a skill, like everything we know, involves more than we can say. (A book that explained everything about bicycle riding would still be unable to teach how to ride a bicycle.) As human nature is social, so is human knowing. And as the achievements of our social nature require authority, so does human knowledge. Epistemic skills are picked up through learning from a master's example, which can occur in a wide variety of places, from classroom to laboratory to workshop. Polanyi writes:

> To learn by example is to submit to authority. You follow your master because you trust his manner of doing things even when you cannot analyse and account in detail for its effectiveness. By watching the master and emulating his efforts in the presence of his example, the apprentice unconsciously picks up the rules of the art, including those which are not explicitly known to the master himself. These hidden rules can be assimilated only by a person who surrenders himself to that extent uncritically to the imitation of another. A society which wants to preserve a fund of personal knowledge must submit to tradition.[23]

One mimics or copies the expert, in order to achieve a like expertise—including the hidden, inarticulate, tacit dimensions of knowledge—that will then become second-nature, something one uses but need not

22 If researchers were truly uncommitted and "objective" nearly 100 per cent of the study of the universe would focus on empty space. For examples of data ignored by researchers, see *Personal Knowledge*, 275f.

23 *Personal Knowledge*, 53.

attend to.[24] Note the claim that the apprentice is learning from the master the rules of the art that include rules "not explicitly known to the master himself." The master does know these rules, but tacitly, not explicitly. The conveyance of tacit knowledge is the achievement of authority. And further, epistemic authority is necessary, and not substitutionary, because there is always tacit knowledge that cannot be articulated explicitly.

Here I see the first necessary function of authority in epistemology. One needs to trust teachers, masters, or experts to have the skills appropriate to the acquisition of knowledge. We may say that this trust goes beyond reason, in that it goes beyond anything that can be said or put in words, yet it is not against reason. Trusting in authority is what social and linguistic animals, social beings with "a fund of personal knowledge," must do if they are to apprehend truth. This conclusion of the necessity of authority is, for Polanyi, not limited to any particular fields of knowledge (e.g., religion or literature); it is true of all knowing whatsoever. Let me underline the paradox. Knowledge—the achievement of the human being, the rational animal—is achieved only by means of a trust in authority that goes beyond reason. Epistemic authority, we find, is located in a place that is beyond or outside reason and yet not against reason.

Still we may go further. As Simon found in society not only an essential function of authority (to determine the means to achieve a good) but also a most essential function (in willing the matter of the common good), so in Polanyi there is not only the necessary function of authority for the artful acquisition of intellectual skills, but also a higher function of authority in the use of those skills by persons of great intelligence. In epistemology as in society, never is the need to trust authority transcended. Quite the contrary: the more an authority a person becomes, the more she must venture trust in others, submitting to their authority.

Say one is starting out in a particular science. The argument has already shown that one must trust experts or connoisseurs in order to acquire the skills of that science, and more broadly in order to achieve competence with regard not only to the articulations of that science's

24 Polanyi distinguishes focal awareness from subsidiary awareness. As an example: it is necessary, in order for me to make a pencil drawing, that I have a subsidiary awareness and not a focal awareness of the pencil in my hand. Our tacit knowledge lies in the realm of which we can (and must) have (only) subsidiary awareness. See *The Tacit Dimension*, 9–10.

explicit knowledge but also as regards its tacit and inarticulable knowledge. Now the argument goes further. We suppose that one at length has become an expert in some field and is no longer an apprentice. One is now, as we say, an authority. However, this does not mean that one is free from needing the authority, the expertise, of others. This deeper argument concerning the necessity of authority focuses on the complexity of knowledge, which provides a practical limit to what any one knower can comprehend. "Indeed," writes Polanyi, "nobody knows more than a tiny fragment of science well enough to judge its validity and value at first hand. For the rest he has to rely on views accepted at second hand on the authority of a community of people accredited as scientists."[25]

We might think at first that an expert can stand free of the authority of others, albeit only with regard to the narrow range of his expertise. But this is to imagine that knowledge is like tiny jewels—hard to obtain, but once I've got one, it's mine. Knowledge, however, does not come in discreet bits like jewels. The expert on the aardvark, for instance, must place his trust in many other zoological experts (not to mention others farther afield) in order for him to be the authority he is. So the very achievement of expertise—which is inseparable from its exercise—requires that one trust and submit to a community of others who have similar, and overlapping, competencies. Because there is no knowledge that is independent of all other knowledge, there is no epistemic authority who stands apart from other epistemic authorities. Experts rely necessarily on the authority of others and cannot do without it. In fact, as knowledge increases, so does the need for submission to authority in the form of the expertise of others.

Polanyi describes this phenomenon under many headings, including tradition, intellectual passions, and "conviviality." The term "conviviality," I believe, is particularly apt for speaking of the inescapably social character of the human being, here focused on "the social dimension of personal knowledge," as Martin Moleski puts it in his perceptive treatment of Polanyi's theological epistemology.[26] Conviviality, indeed as the word suggests, is a joyous sharing of life together, including the life of culture, of language, of seeking truth. A "*previous act of affiliation*," Polanyi writes, is necessary for the transmission of culture, including language, wisdom, values, and so forth. By such an act of affiliation, a person submits to the authority of "a community which

25 *Personal Knowledge*, 163.

26 Moleski, *Personal Catholicism*, 83.

cultivates this lore."[27] Affiliation, which begins in apprenticeship but continues throughout the lives even of experts, consists in decisions to trust authorities, decisions that are "inevitable," "unceasing," and "comprehensive."[28] These decisions place one within a social framework, a social structure of authority. The personal act, which underlies any acquisition of knowledge, is necessarily one of social identification and trust, an acceptance of authority that will grow, not diminish, within a structure of conviviality.

In short, the high functioning of epistemic authority permits an individual to take a place within a social structure of authority, by having expertise upon some small slice of the knowledge of how things are. Only by trusting others and sharing convivially can any one person rise to become, and continue to be, an authority in some matter. This trust in others is not substitutionary, for no human being can ever grow out of it.

As social authority is for the sake of free persons, so is epistemic authority for the sake of knowing persons. This brings us anew to "an essential qualification" that must be added to our account of epistemic authority.[29] Affiliation, conviviality, apprenticeship, ongoing submission to the authority of others—none of it is an act of unquestioned acceptance. For authority never functions without drawing forth a response. Polanyi says that "every thoughtful submission to authority is qualified by some, however slight, opposition to it."[30] This is because the end is not authority, but the knowledge of truth. That is, truth is not for the sake of authority, but authority for the sake of truth. Thus does science advance: not by leaving authority behind, but by the adepts of science asking, particularly in their own fields of expertise, whether the conclusions, practices, and convictions of what we might call the scientific community are true. We must see here two things. First, since we never become individuals who escape from conviviality, it is impossible to ask the question of truth without a continuing submission to authority. But second and conversely, it is impossible to submit to authority without asking the question of truth.[31]

27 *Personal Knowledge*, 207; emphasis original.

28 Ibid., 209.

29 Ibid., 208.

30 Ibid., 164.

31 This is the kernel of truth half-captured in the slogan "Question Authority." When authority is submitted to, by that very submission there is a note of question. The slogan should be: "Joyfully submit to authority even as you question it"—but that's too long for a bumper sticker.

Epistemic authority, in sum, is grounded in the personal character of knowledge, which itself is connected to the tacit element in anything that is known. Epistemic authority is needed for something like apprenticeship, the acquisition of skills and lore and understandings that go beyond what can be articulated in full. It initiates the knower into a society of authorities, each of whom needs the others, as people who seek to discover, in increasingly comprehensive ways yet never irrefutably final, the truth about the world and the things in it.

Objections

Aquinas would teach us that we cannot understand an argument if we are not able to see the objections that could be made against it. In accordance with this old wisdom, I again give what seem to me three significant objections to the account I have just made of epistemic authority.

Objection 1. The key illustration of a judge coming to a decision is presented as if the range of possible judgments always narrows down unequivocally to a single possibility. Why should we assume that is true? Chapter 2 argued that, as regards social authority, the more human we are, the more free we are, and thus the more we need authority to make choices among equally good alternatives. If the conductor is not drawn to the single, true, best, and only possible performance, why is the judge drawn to find a uniquely correct judgment? Polanyi may be right to describe reality as the external lure and anchor of the human quest for knowledge. But why should we assume that the experts, the authorities, get so close as to be able to see reality in clear focus, even granted the limitation of view to a narrow field only? Perhaps, again given human finitude, it is only rare to reach such a position. Perhaps most of the time the vision of the expert also remains fuzzy, and thus the expert in fact does act arbitrarily: he comes to the limit of what he can understand, and then must use his will, his arbitrary will, to finalize his verdict.

Objection 2. The argument has repeatedly stated that, if one wishes to know, it is necessary to submit to authority. But we should not celebrate the notion of submission. Many historical tragedies have risen from the unwillingness of persons to question authority as they should have. Social, structural sins—one thinks of racism, sexism, and the like—can be addressed only when individuals refuse to submit to them. We need brave individuals who will question authority in order to overcome systemic injustices.

Objection 3. Authorities may be helpful, but they also get in the way of truth. They pass along error and prejudice as part of culture, insight, and values. That is why we need to encourage independent thinkers who challenge what is received as wisdom.

These are significant objections, and it seems to me that each of them is partially correct.

Reply to objection 1. I can see no reason in principle to say that an expert is always able, through persistent application of her intellectual skills, to attain a univocally given answer to the question at hand. There can be no question that just as there are bad performances, so there are bad judgments. Perhaps conversely, just as there is no single best performance, so there is no single best judgment. But we are on shakier ground, I think, when we describe what the judge then does as an act of her arbitrary will. She does not think to herself, "My judgment cannot be A or B, but it could be C, D, or E, and so I'll choose C as an expression of my arbitrary will." We go back to her subjective experience, which is the experience of anyone who is seeking to know. She feels herself drawn or lured by reality, and she has made a commitment to follow that draw, that lure. Success may not be forthcoming in any given case, but that does not change what is sought. Furthermore, as a well-practiced, skilled person in her field, she carries with her a body of tacit knowledge. So when she issues a verdict that goes beyond what her reason can articulate, it may nevertheless be a verdict of knowledge, not of (mere) will.

Reply to objection 2. It would be foolish to deny that harm has indeed been done by people who should have questioned authority. But if our argument is correct that epistemic authority is necessary for us as humans, then the denial of that necessity will itself also cause harm. That is to say, if in fact the way of apprenticeship, obedience, and submission is the way one must take in coming to knowledge, then to deny that fact will encourage cultural impoverishment, a reduction in what we are able to understand and appreciate, a narrowing of the range of the human. But despite this, the objection rightly points out the necessity of understanding the relation of authority to error. And while the argument already has pointed out that the truth to which authority points raises inevitably, if only (generally) in some small way, a question that turns back on the authority—which is to say that the argument "builds in" a moment in which we "question authority"—nonetheless the question of error does need further development, which I will attempt to provide in Chapter 6.

Reply to objection 3. The response here is similar to that given in the previous paragraph. Authorities can and sometimes do get in the way of truth. Nonetheless, if "independent thinking" (conceived as an activity deliberately apart from tradition, culture, or community) is a chimera, then to encourage it cannot be to encourage a real human good. What we need to understand is truthful thinking that can question authority while at the same time appreciating its necessary and positive functions in human knowing.

Let us now circle back to the judge of our initial illustration.[32] When she arrives at her judgment, she presents it to the world as true, that is to say, as universally valid. She puts it forth as the judgment that any judge in her place should have made. She must assert it confidently—it is, indeed, her responsibility to do so.[33] But once issued, her judgment will be tested. Other judges will exercise their intellectual capacities to decide whether the verdict in this case deserves to be a precedent for similar cases. Through a web of such decisions, mutually interlocking in the judgments of competent authorities, broader and broader assertions of truth are made possible. Reality is an external anchor of our commitment, but reality is hidden.

Meanwhile, the individual who seeks to know the truth—whether that individual be a judge, a researcher, an artisan, or whoever—cannot live in isolation. Authorities function "convivially," which means under authority. Polanyi's careful, detailed, and comprehensive account of personal knowledge allows us to see how authority is essential to human knowing. Nonetheless, authority, albeit necessary for grasping truth, can never guarantee that truth has been grasped. The truth which authority helps uncover, and preserve, and pass on to others, and which includes inarticulable tacit elements—that truth itself circles back to raise a question about authority. This simply is the mode

32 For the background of which, see Polanyi, *Personal Knowledge*, 308–16.

33 Knowers are members of a society of discoverers, according to Polanyi's student Richard Gelwick. "In relying on the clues given to us [by tradition and inquiry], we cannot strictly assure that we shall be right. Our knowing is a search for the truth through the matrix of our existence.... We are not free to do as we please but called to respond to the clues and problems that can be ascertained by us and other competent persons. Our satisfaction is not in pleasing ourselves but in our contact with aspects of reality that can be found by others and offer prospect of further discovery." Gelwick, *The Way of Discovery*, 76.

in which human beings have and share knowledge. It may seem tragic that infallibility eludes us. But a contrary view might be entertained as well. If to be human is to be the linguistic animal, a body that talks with and lives with others in society, then it may not be our burden that we need authority, it may be the glory of our nature.

The Paradoxes of Human Knowing

The purpose of his book *Personal Knowledge*, according to Polanyi, was "to achieve a frame of mind in which I may hold firmly to what I believe to be true, even though I know that it might conceivably be false."[34] It is necessary that we assert what we come to know as something that is true; our assertion, Polanyi also says, is made necessarily with universal intent. But at the same time we cannot help but be aware that, upon further investigation, what we assert as true may need to be understood in a new way, or even rejected. We may turn out to have been wrong. Herein are paradoxes of human knowing.[35]

If I have come to know something, then I understand it as something that is the case quite apart from my assertion of its truth. That a certain strain of bacterium causes illness in humans is a truth about the world, and is asserted by a scientist with universal validity. It isn't true just because the scientist says so; nor is it the kind of thing which might be referred to as "my truth," that is, it's true for me but might not be for you. Likewise for a judgment that a certain act of violence was murder, or that powdered yeast can be dissolved in such a way as to leaven the whole lump. These judgments are not put forth as instances of "my truth" but rather, as Polanyi says, with universal intent.

But given the possibility of error, which can never be eliminated, one might think it better to avoid categorical assertions and make conditional assertions only. Could we not always calibrate our statements with a declaration of the degree of probability attached to them? Such was endeavored by the scholastic manuals of Roman Catholic theology in the period preceding Vatican II. In these manuals, a note

34 *Personal Knowledge*, 214.

35 If this were a longer book, I would take up the epistemology of John Henry Newman (1801–90). Newman's "illative sense"—the name comes from the Latin *fero*, "to carry"—is the human capacity to understand beyond the deliverances of reason, to draw true inferences. There are striking parallels between Newman's thought and Polanyi's, but no evidence that the latter was aware of the former. For a clear treatment, see Moleski, *Personal Catholicism.*

was attached to each statement of a theological truth; the note indicated, in Avery Dulles's words, "the degree of certitude and emphasis attaching to the thesis."[36] By extension, could we not proportion our assent to the probability of the proposition we are asserting? If something is likely to be true but possibly false, why must I assert it (if I assert it) with commitment that it is true? Why not just give it a partial assertion?

Upon examination, this proposal turns out to be impossible. Suppose, instead of asserting X, I tried to assert something like, "I hold X to be true with a 75% likelihood." But by making this change all I have done is change what it is that I am asserting. Instead of asserting X, I am now asserting a new statement; let's call it X2. The statement X2 is simply, "I hold X to be true with a 75% likelihood." In other words, I have changed *what* I am asserting, not the *probability with which* I am asserting it. That which I am asserting—the new statement X2—I am indeed asserting wholly. The alternative leads us to the trap of an infinite regress. If every statement needs an attached note to indicate the degree of probability with which it is asserted, then X2 also needs a note indicating its own degree of probability. The result would be that while I thought I was solving a problem, I would have instead introduced a whole new, unending series of problems. With each new, reformulated statement (X3, X4, etc.), I must make a further assertion that incorporates the degree of probability of the new statement. Unfortunately, I will never be able to complete this task, and thus, if every assertion must be a probabilistic assertion, I will never be able to assert anything at all.

Yet in reality, we make assertions all the time. Each sentence that I am writing is an assertion, and I put each one before you with an implicit claim of universal validity. It might be that my original statement X was naive or lacking in nuance, that X2 is actually a better statement. But all that means is that a wiser person would assert X2 rather than X.

We "must forever try to discover knowledge that will stand up by itself," as Polanyi says in a passage quoted earlier. Yet whatever we discover, we assert without a probabilistic qualification: for, upon reflection, we catch ourselves "red-handed in the act of upholding [our] knowledge."[37] Since we live convivially, there will be a dialectic within which statements of truth are ventured, often received, sometimes

36 Dulles, *The Craft of Theology*, 41–2.

37 Polanyi, *The Study of Man*, 11–12.

rejected, frequently modified, continually incorporated into a larger understanding, until at length new statements of truth are put forward. The point to grasp is that every assertion within this process is made by one who is committed to truth and who holds to what he is asserting as, simply, true. On the assumption of good will and integrity, there is no other way to make statements about the way things are.

Another strategy that we might consider adopting in order to avoid making false assertions is to limit our assertions to "core truths," and to eschew assertions about non-essentials. This is the strategy behind what we sometimes find in Lutheran, Anglican, and other protestant sources: the notion that some claims of theology are less-important *adiaphora.* There are, it is asserted, core doctrines, things which a given church must say and which, thus, cannot be compromised for some other purpose—social justice perhaps, or ecumenical advance.[38] For instance, although to secure greater Christian unity Anglicans might be willing to part with *adiaphora* like "the flutter of surplices" or the cadences of the traditional Book of Common Prayer, they have not been willing to jettison bishops or communion wine. These latter items are said to belong to core doctrine, the remainder being *adiaphora*—matters of relative indifference. This distinction seems clear enough. But one can ask (I once found the Anglican process theologian Norman Pittinger asking[39]): is the distinction of core doctrine from *adiaphora* itself a core doctrine or not? Now things are not so clear. It would seem that the idea—that core doctrine is separable from other matters—could not itself be a matter of core doctrine. It would be an odd claim to elevate to the level of the eternal generation of the Son from the Father. But

38 With regard to the contemporary Anglican disputes over whether Christian marriage can be extended to persons of the same sex, Ephraim Radner interestingly holds that disputants on all sides share the same mind set: that one can know, in advance of discussion, what are the core essentials of Christian faith and what are inessential matters. For the liberals in this discussion, the core may be simply the Nicene Creed. A slightly wider view would include the items of the Chicago-Lambeth Quadrilateral. The radical conservatives have a more capacious core that includes not only these items but also typically the Thirty-Nine Articles and the text and rubrics of the 1662 Book of Common Prayer (and perhaps other "standards"). All parties make the same error, and consequently find themselves trapped in fruitless debate over the true elements of the core. See Ephraim Radner and Philip Turner, *The Fate of Communion: The Agony of Anglicanism and the Future of a Global Church* (Grand Rapids, Mich.: Eerdmans, 2006), 91–2.

39 He put it along the lines of: is the distinction between a necessary truth and an optional truth itself a necessary truth or an optional truth?

if the distinction is not core doctrine, then we could presumably do without the distinction.

Such considerations have led me to the view that we are not capable of specifying, explicitly and infallibly, the essential points of Christian doctrine, although I have no doubt that the Trinity is essential and surplices, although quintessentially Anglican, are not. As a theologian, I desire to know the essential truths of the Christian faith, and it is those truths that I wish to affirm. But I cannot thereby foreclose the possibility of error in any specific explicit assertion I might make. We cannot escape this paradox at the heart of all human knowing (and certainly not only in matters of faith). We are personally committed whenever we assert something as true; at the same time, we assert it as truly being knowledge about the way things are independently of our coming to know. We cannot but assert it with universal intent; nonetheless, we may prove to have been wrong.

It is proper to refer to human knowing as entailing paradox. Recall that a paradox is a complex claim that we cannot grasp all together (e.g., light acts like a wave and light acts like a series of particles). It is paradox because, although we cannot grasp it entire, we have good reason to hold each part of the complex claim (light acts like a wave; light acts like a series of particles) and the claims together do not contradict each other (we have equations which express the reality of light and they don't self-destruct as contradictions). With regard to human knowing, we have reason to believe each of the following claims: it involves personal commitment; it really is knowledge; it is made with universal intent; any statement of it may prove erroneous. These claims do not fit within the usual and comfortable disjunctions of everyday thought (subjectivity vs. objectivity, relativism vs. universalism, and the like). We cannot see how they fit together. Nonetheless, they do actually fit together, in that this is how human knowledge is. And as Aristotle is credited with saying, if it's actual, it's possible (i.e., it's not a contradiction).

The late Thomas Kuhn in his study of the structure of scientific revolutions introduced a term into popular currency: "paradigm shift." Like Polanyi, Kuhn took aim at the idea that scientists are indifferent to the data that comes before them, that they are uncommitted in their investigations, and that they do nothing except simply draw the conclusions that the data provide. On the contrary, said Kuhn, most of the time scientists work within an accepted "paradigm" of their field. The paradigm tells them what to expect, and the business of "ordinary science" is to work out the implications and fill in the details to complete the picture given by the paradigm.[40] But sometimes data will appear that don't fit within the regnant paradigm. Initially such data will be ignored, on the plausible assumption that future investigations will explain away their (apparent) inconsistency with the paradigm. But if they refuse to go away, are continually repeated, and no way is found to reconcile the data with the paradigm; if, in addition, other non-fitting data accumulate in other parts of the paradigm; then, finally, the paradigm itself gives way, "shifts," and we have a scientific revolution. After the revolution, a new paradigm emerges triumphant, and ordinary science takes over, solving unsolved problems within the new paradigm.

Scientists are committed to their paradigms, so much so that, while they work within them, they are not able fully to articulate what it is that they are assuming. Kuhn's work is misunderstood if it is taken as an argument against scientific method or as a summons not to accept working within a paradigm. Science and knowledge and, in general, all seeking after truth is done within a paradigm and, in fact, could not be carried on without it. At the moment of the revolution, there is not a paradigm-free paradise of free inquiry. And hence the paradox. Scientific advance, the search for truth, is premised on the submission to a paradigm which, in the long run, may prove inadequate to reality. Yet scientists do not doubtfully assume their current paradigm; they take it on, in part explicitly, in part tacitly, and in general wholeheartedly.

Polanyi developed the concepts of "indwelling" and "framework" to speak of this characteristic of human knowing. We indwell a conceptual framework, which will do such things for us as determine facts and methods of inquiry and suggest lines of research, and we can be conscious of our indwelling. We will, in fact, employ our interpretive framework (as Moleski says) "to reach definite decisions." Nonetheless (now quoting Polanyi himself), "The curious thing is that we have no clear knowledge of what our presuppositions are and when we try to formulate them they appear quite unconvincing." These paradoxes accepted, it is also the case that we are not trapped within a framework

40 Polanyi's 1946 work, *Science, Faith, and Society*, spoke of scientific "intuition," which he later "described as the tacit coefficient of a scientific theory," by which a theory "foresees yet indeterminate manifestations of the experience on which it bears." Moleski, *Personal Catholicism*, 54, quoting from Polanyi's 1963 introduction to a republication of this earlier work. Moleski also tells us that, in that introduction, Polanyi "claims that his approach to the philosophy of science is much like that of," among others, "Thomas Kuhn."

of understanding. Paradigms can be shifted, and are. Polanyi ascribes a role for intellectual passions in these shifts.[41]

Here are two pictures, on different levels, of indwelling a framework. The members of an academic community exercise epistemic authority through peer-reviewed journals, accreditation of institutions, the bestowal of tenure, the granting of degrees, and so forth. Such authority is necessary, and must be exercised within a commitment to truth that nonetheless cannot guarantee freedom from error. On a different level altogether, we must necessarily assume that our senses, by which we apprehend the world, do indeed apprehend *the world*, and do so with fundamental truthfulness, despite whatever limitations and filters they impose. If we do not assume this, then we are doomed to be able to say nothing about anything except ourselves. It is a paradox that our knowledge (at least our non-introspective knowledge) is based on senses which cannot guarantee their own truthfulness.

So the paradoxes of knowledge are always with us. At times we do reach contradictions in our thought. When a contradiction presses upon us and refuses to be resolved by means, say, of a distinction (when, that is, I'm forced to say that Fred really is both fully a man and fully a duck), then we must go back to the beginning and reexamine our initial assumptions. This is very clear in geometry. Euclid proves a number of theorems by first assuming their opposite. Then he draws out the necessary consequences of that assumption until he reaches something that is a contradiction to known reality. The contradiction *cannot be*, and therefore the initial assumption was wrong. And therefore the theorem is true.

Outside pure mathematics, it may not be immediately clear what the faulty assumption was, nor may it be altogether certain that we have a contradiction. In many cases we are confronted with an argument that, while seemingly consistent with itself, seems also to be arbitrary and burdensomely complex in terms of what it intends to explain. Conspiracy theories are often that way: it is impossible to argue someone out of one, for he already has an account for any point you bring up. "Bush did it for oil" says a sticker you can see, as I'm writing this, on lampposts and bus stops in New York. Alongside the words are the Twin Towers with smoke rising from them, and the insinuation is that the U.S. President was behind the devastating attacks of September

41 This discussion quotes directly and otherwise draws upon the argument made by Moleski, *Personal Catholicism*, 81. The direct quote from Polanyi is from *Personal Knowledge*, 59.

2001. A person who believes that is not a person you can reason with, even though there may be no internal contradiction in his thought.

Which is to say that not only is human knowing paradoxical, it is also subtle. This leads us back from paradox to authority. Epistemic authority is for our good, as it teaches us not only a body of knowledge but also a body of skills and tacit understandings. And it tests and possibly incorporates our personal knowledge into broader understandings. A mind may be thoroughly consistent and free of contradictions and yet be very small. Such a mind lacks authority. Epistemic authority is a broadening gift to a society of human beings.

You Shall Know the Truth and the Truth Shall Make You Free

"*I believe that in spite of the hazards involved, I am called upon to search for the truth and state my findings.*" Polanyi offers this sentence as a summary of his "fiduciary programme." It has as its content his "ultimate belief." Yet it is also something that he asserts. "[I]n uttering this sentence I both say that I must commit myself by thought and speech, and do so at the same time." The sentence thus demonstrates that epistemological enquiry has an intentional circularity.[42]

That circularity is embedded in a person. As with social authority, so here: it is in a living person that epistemic authority comes to us. An authoritative judgment, as in the illustration early in this chapter, is an unqualified assertion of the truth by an authority who has gone searching for it. She will aim to declare the truth particularly as it is hard to discern for those who lack the authoritative expertise. But truth is never severed from the need that authority have a hand in the grasping of it. That is to say, truth, however much it may seem to stand on its own objectively, never escapes from some human being who is holding it.

By leading us to truth, and by locating our own judgments in wider knowledge, epistemic authority offers the good of liberation from error and impotence while integrating us into the society of knowers. That word "knowers" is not ironic, but it is synonymous with another word: "seekers." For to have knowledge is to have felt the lure for truth and to have committed oneself thereto. And whatever we may know, we know it only as persons within an interconnected web of other knowers, and

42 *Personal Knowledge*, 299.

thus seekers, a community of authorities who challenge, test, validate, qualify, and incorporate one another's assertions of truth.

For the ultimate claim of personal epistemic authority we may turn to Christian theology. In St. John's Gospel, Jesus says, "Ye shall know the truth, and the truth shall make you free" (8.32). It is clear that Jesus, in this passage, speaking of the truth, is speaking of himself. He has said, "If ye continue in my word, then are ye my disciples indeed; and ye shall know the truth..." (8.31f.). To continue in Jesus' word is to continue in what he teaches. He also says, "I am the way, the truth..." (14.6). So to continue in Jesus' word is to continue in Jesus himself, and that is to be in the truth. In Christianity the truth not only comes to us as a person who speaks with authority, the truth is that person, the one is authorized by his Father to speak as he does (cf. 14.10).

Theology suggests, then, that the fullest sense of knowing comes from the commitment of the one who would know to the one who is authorized by his Father. And this knowledge, theology further suggests, is truly liberating. For it is equivalent to being "in Jesus," which is to say "in" the one fully human being. One is liberated here into full humanity, and that, as we saw in Chapter 2, is found in our living together.

Polanyi sees belief as inextricably part of his epistemology. Tongue in cheek, he claims Augustine (who had lived more than a thousand years before the rise of "critical" philosophy) as the first "post-critical" philosopher, the progenitor of the project that Polanyi took up in *Personal Knowledge*. For it was Augustine who said, *nisi credideritis, non intelligitis*: you do not understand, if you have not first believed.[43] The theological suggestion that we have seen in St. John's Gospel is only that: a suggestion, a sketch of an argument. Nevertheless, the gospel words serve as a confirmation of sorts to our philosophical conclusions, that knowledge requires submission to epistemic authority, and that the truth we can attain only by means of that authority is deeply congruent with the freedom that we attain only by means of social authority.

43 Ibid., 266. The Augustine quotation comes from his treatise *De libero arbitrio*.

Chapter 4

AUTHORITY AND POWER: POLITICAL AUTHORITY

Our Depoliticized Imagination

The first difficulty in discussing political authority is in admitting there is such a thing.

When Eugene Kennedy and Sara Charles write that authority is "the most misunderstood idea in America," they premise their diagnosis on a sharp distinction between authority and authoritarianism.[1] The distinction hangs on the use of force. Contrary to popular belief, they say, real authority "augments" the human, and has nothing to do with coercive force, which, they think necessarily, diminishes the human. Authoritarianism, by their contrast, has to do precisely with the employment of force, and thus is the opposite of real authority. These authors draw on the Latin root of authority, *augere*, which is "to augment," or more generally, to cause to increase, to grow. They offer concrete prescriptions for the recovery of authority in various arenas of American life, including the home, the self, education, work, the professions, and the institutions of government, business, religion, and the law. Behind all their prescriptions is a summons to reclaim personal authority, which they also call moral authority. But this reclamation project cannot be a return to hierarchical authority, they say, because of deep changes in society. Authority cannot be top-down, and, in any event, all top-down authority is implicitly coercive (and thus in opposition to the

1 Eugene Kennedy and Sara C. Charles, *Authority: The Most Misunderstood Idea in America* (New York: The Free Press, 1997).

true character of authority). In the present-day world, authority must be radically decentralized and person-centered.

While I agree (as the reader will see in subsequent chapters) that in the end authority has to do with the authorization of the individual, I do not think we can get to that end apart from political authority—as, seemingly, Kennedy and Charles think we can. Their book exemplifies the depoliticized imagination that characterizes much contemporary thought. Besides their bold subtitle, "The Most Misunderstood Idea in America," Kennedy and Charles employ as an epigraph a bracing quotation from Simon's *General Theory of Authority*: "The issue of authority has such a bad reputation that a philosopher cannot discuss it without exposing himself to suspicion and malice. Yet authority is present in all phases of social life. . . . Why is it that men distrust so intensely a thing without which they cannot, by all evidences, live and act together?"[2] This epigraph, unfortunately, is the last time Simon appears in their pages; its appearance presages neither an engagement with Simon's thought nor a bold philosophical attack on the ideas that Americans hold. Rather than recovering an awareness of the need for authority in order to make determinations about the means and willing of the common good—a project, as I will show below, that entails an appreciation of the use of political power—Kennedy and Charles limit their argument, instead, to the non-political psychology of individuals. They do not lack the courage to point out widespread cultural mistakes, such as the assumption that "empowerment" is the key to all good in intimate relations. Authority has a place in intimacy, they assert counter-culturally; authority "is an open and freeing agency of relationship, while power is a competitive striving for franchise rights."[3] But such counter-cultural thrusts as they make rest on a deeper, and unexamined, acceptance of the modern depoliticized imagination, which signally manifests itself in their unquestioning distrust of power.

The authority that Kennedy and Charles summon us to reclaim has its source inside us. "*Real authority—the capacity to author their marriages and families successfully—lies, like the Kingdom of God, within people themselves.*"[4] Here they link their depoliticized authority with

2 Simon, *A General Theory of Authority*, 13. Kennedy and Charles slightly misquote Simon. The contemporary situation differs from Simon's in the respect that, in circles of legal philosophy, there is much discussion of the purpose and legitimacy of forceful political authority. See, for example, *Authority*, ed. Joseph Raz (New York: New York University Press, 1990).

3 Kennedy and Charles, *Authority*, 33.

4 Ibid., 57; emphasis original.

a characteristically depoliticized theology, about which I will say more shortly. But if authority is within us, how can there be political authority?

Kennedy and Charles devote about nine pages to the "de-authorization" of the "institution" of government. Here they attribute the disorderly style of the Clinton administration to the anti-authoritarian atmosphere in which the president and his contemporaries came to maturity. They speak of the lack of transparency in the failed health-care project of 1993. They speak of the confusions of the Speaker of the House and Clinton's leading opponent, Newt Gingrich, who seemed to understand the radical change from centralized authority to the new reality of "devolution," but who at the same time did not seem to grasp that true authority (personal, natural, moral) is not the same as a content-indifferent managerialism.[5] All this is doubtless true, and provides an insightful analysis of American governmental dysfunctions of the 1990s. But it does not take us deep. It does not, for instance, help us understand what is distinctive about the political realm. It does not help us understand power, or the relationship of power and authority, or indeed the nature of political authority.

Yet these authors are hardly alone, for the depoliticization of the modern imagination is nigh ubiquitous. One can find it even in the high towers of the Vatican. We may take the late and undeniably worthy Pope John Paul II as an example. It would be hard to overstate John Paul's influence on the politics of the latter part of the twentieth century. Nonetheless, his instincts were ever to edit out the political import of the Christian message. For instance, there is a long tradition of understanding Christ as having three functions or offices, namely, prophet, priest, and king. John Paul had much to say about Christ as prophet and priest, but when he wrote about Christ's kingly function, he limited it to Christ's self-rule; he never spoke of Christ as ruling over the universe, the world, the leaders of the nations, and so forth. John Paul didn't make a point of saying Christ *didn't* rule over them. But he did not teach or speak about Christ's kingly rule in such terms. Rather, Christ's kingship was exemplified in his complete self-mastery; he ruled over himself so that he would be free to serve others. There was a moral point to this teaching of John Paul's: each Christian should so exercise self-discipline, self-rule, that he or she is free to serve others. Gone is the political point of Christ's kingship, made forcefully, for example, by Pope Pius XI when he established the annual solemnity of

5 Ibid., 183–92.

Christ the King in 1925.[6] In John Paul's handling, Christ's kingship has become self-rule for the sake of service.[7]

Thus on the one hand the American psychologist and medical doctor couple of Kennedy and Charles, and on the other hand the Vicar of Christ John Paul II, both exemplify the personalization and depoliticization of contemporary thought. But the interior Kingdom of God, self-rule for the sake of service, hardly exhausts the biblical and theological, not to mention papal, tradition of Christ's kingship. Yes, the kingdom of God is "within you," Jesus said (at least according to Lk. 17.21 in the classic Authorized or King James Version).[8] But he is reported also to have said that the Son of Man would come to judge the nations, and would separate them, and would pronounce condemnation on the "goats" (Mt. 25.31–46). The first epistle to the Corinthians tells us that the rule of all the nations will be placed at his feet (15.24–8). And we have seen in Chapter 2 that the biblical notion of authority is an integrated one, with all authority coming from God and all authorities finding themselves both in and under authority that is ultimately from God.

My argument is that just as we need social and epistemic authority, so we cannot do without political authority. The argument is in part biblical and theological: if we can overcome our anti-political presuppositions, we will see that the Christian texts and traditions are saturated with political understanding. The fundamental insight to be found here entails a distinction between political authority per se

6 Pius XI, *Quas primas*. The text, with English translation, may be found on the official Vatican website www.vatican.va. A standard source for the English translations of papal encyclicals of this period is Claudia Carlen, ed., *The Papal Encyclicals (1740–1981)*, 5 vols. (Wilmington, N.C.: McGrath, 1981); for *Quas primas* see 4.273–9.

7 For a broad development of this thesis, see Victor Lee Austin, "A Christological Social Vision: The Uses of Christ in the Social Encyclicals of John Paul II," Ph.D. dissertation (Fordham University, 2002). See also Victor Lee Austin, "John Paul II's Ironic Legacy in Political Theology," *Pro Ecclesia* 16 (2007): 165–94. Avery Dulles accepted the point and incorporated it as a tension between John Paul's teaching and the tradition of the church. See Avery Cardinal Dulles, "John Paul II and the Mystery of the Human Person," in *Church and Society: The Laurence J. McGinley Lectures, 1988–2007* (New York: Fordham University Press, 2008), 425, 428 n. 20.

8 This verse is a unique Gospel instance of Jesus saying the kingdom of God is "*entos*" you (with a plural "you"). *Entos* is, we are told, a rare adverb of place. In this verse it may indeed refer to spiritual interiority; yet, alternatively, it may refer to the kingdom as being "among you" or "in your midst." For discussion, see Joseph A. Fitzmyer, *The Gospel According to Luke*, The Anchor Bible (Garden City, N.Y.: Doubleday, 1985), 2.1160–1.

and political authority in the historical period between Christ's ascension and his return to establish his kingdom. According to the former, political authority has three elements, namely, power, judgment, and the perpetuation of tradition, all held together in one agency. But in the period following the triumph of Christ (his resurrection and ascension), a secular political authority has come into existence whose chastened and limited purpose is simply to protect the right.

The argument is also philosophical. Political authority is related to the kinds of authority we have already examined; particularly, it may be seen as social authority at its most extensive. And here it is that power must be accounted for. In Chapter 2 we spoke of social authority in the context of a plurality of societies, "mini-societies," which overlap one another in various complex ways. But social authority at its most extensive, which is to say the authority that is for the society as a whole (which is what we mean by political authority): this authority has no (human) social authority beyond itself. Thus political authority must have recourse to coercive force in order to deal with violence, recalcitrance, and many other effects of sin. (Other social authorities, at the limit, can only exclude. A business fires an intractable employee; a string quartet decides the violist needs to play elsewhere. If coercion is needed, these social authorities appeal for it from beyond themselves, namely, from political authority.) Were there no sin, political authority *would still exist* but would not need in any way to coerce the support and cooperation of citizens. That is to say, finitude alone, while it calls for authority, does not call for coercion; and political authority, while it must have power, need not have coercive force at its disposal. And even in the presence of sin, for most of its ongoing, everyday exercise political authority does not function by compulsion but by assent—always, however, with the threat that compulsion may be brought upon those who defy it.[9]

9 The consideration of sinless humans is a heuristic device; in this world, we will always have to deal with sin. This is not an argument that any existing government could do away with coercive force. Thus it is not a disagreement with the defense of government's coercive power made by John Rawls: "[E]ven in a well-ordered society the coercive powers of government are to some degree necessary for the stability of social cooperation. For although men know that they share a common sense of justice and that each wants to adhere to the existing arrangements, they may nevertheless lack full confidence in one another. . . . [T]he existence of effective penal machinery serves as men's security to one another." John Rawls, *A Theory of Justice* (Cambridge, Mass.: Harvard University Press, 1971), 240. Rawls calls this Hobbes's thesis; it is based on a mistrust of fellow citizens. If the mistrust is warranted, then sin exists; if not warranted, then the mistrust itself is a species of sin.

What is political authority for? Since the human good is to live together in free communications, political authority exists for that good. But it is not the initiator or the creator of the human good, nor is the political realm simply equivalent to the public realm. One recalls Simon's teaching that the more advanced a society is, the more it requires government—government *qua* that specialized function that attends to the good of the whole, in concrete and changing circumstances, so that other persons may attend to the good, not in utter privacy, but in important public fields that nonetheless are not as extensive as the common good of the whole.

My argument, in short, is that political authority has a robust theological interpretation, and that it follows with a consistency of argument from social and epistemic authority. When we speak of authority, politics is not the first thing we should speak of. But neither can we speak of authority without speaking of politics. I will try now to make the argument more concrete by examining the exercise of political judgment.

Illustration: An Exercise of Political Judgment

A wrong has been done and the wrong-doer has been brought to court for judgment. The matter would seem to be straightforward; the court needs but to assure itself of the facts and then apply the punishment. But there are complexities.

That a wrong has been done will, normally, not be a matter of dispute. But it does fall to the court to state with clarity what the wrong was. The taxi-driver who ran into the pedestrian, was his wrong that he was driving too fast, or speeding through a yellow light, or talking on his cell phone? Did he accelerate when he saw her in his way? Does it matter to the description of the wrong that the pedestrian was outside the crosswalk? Does it matter that she was a violist just laid off by her orchestra, and that she faces an uncertain future on account of her shoulder that was fractured when the taxi hit her? The description of the wrong needs to define clearly what has occurred; the ability to make such a description is, we know from the previous chapter, an exercise of epistemic authority: an apprehension of the truth of the matter. The description needs to be clear and accurate because the injured person, as well as the one who caused the injury, and also the society at large are all interested parties who need and deserve to have the truth told. It takes epistemic authority to see and state the truth.

In addition to the pronouncement of guilt, which includes truthful description of what has been done, the court will issue a punishment. This also is a complex matter, which the laws recognize by giving judges discretion in sentencing. Mitigating factors may be at play, both in the event when the wrong occurred but also in the circumstances under which the punishment will be carried out. The driver's need for livelihood, the violist's need for the same, the consequences for the city of a sentence that is perceived as excessively harsh or, alternatively, so light as to be unserious—these are elements that come into play, although none of them may be determinative.

In both parts of judgment, the statement of the wrong and the execution of the punishment, the court is required to look in two directions. And that is because the act of judgment is always both backward-looking and forward-looking. It looks to the past not only to make a verdict on wrong, but to put an end to the wrong that has happened, to bring a close to the unhappy event and to foreclose possible future revenge. So both the verdict and the sentence of punishment have that backward-looking aspect. They also both look forward, to the future which they now help establish. In this society in the future it will now be known, by the authoritative political judgment that has been issued, that the action in question was indeed wrong. Political judgment articulates the order of a society even as it buttresses and shapes that order, carrying it into the future. And it is into that future that the injured party now must live. She cannot ask for further compensation or revenge, but needs to accept the judgment as the gift of closure that it is. And the wrong-doer must accept the wrong he has done, and pay the penalty imposed as a necessary yet also sufficient condition of his continuance in his political society.

This illustration shows how an everyday judgment of a court is a political judgment. The same bidirectionality is characteristic of decisions of legislatures and political executives. To decide to build a public library is a judgment that makes pronouncement upon the past and looks to shape the future. To repair a sewage problem, to recognize and address the scarcity of public transit in areas of poverty, to provide a system of courts, to anticipate the information needed by government agencies in order to counter an emerging terrorist network: each of these is an exercise in judgment, an implicit pronouncement upon a wrong or defect (whether deliberately caused or not), and a provision to establish the right for the future.

Political judgment thus involves social authority, the determination of the means to attain the common good of a society and the material willing of that common good. And political judgment involves epistemic authority, the commitment and the skills to seek the truth. But it also involves power, the ability to impose a sentence, or command the payment of taxes, or direct the expenditure of funds, or regulate activities. It is this employment of power, combined with a care for the good of the given society as a whole and informed by epistemic authority, that makes political authority distinctive. We cannot speak of politics without speaking of power.

So if there is such a thing as political authority, then Kennedy and Charles are wrong to divorce authority and power, and John Paul's Christology is defective insofar as it does not speak of Christ as having power over other authorities. But what is the power that is appropriate to political authority? That is to say, what is the nature of this authority that we call political? Since our cultural presuppositions are politically impoverished, the way forward will require an exercise in theological retrieval.

Political Authority

The liberation theology of the latter part of the twentieth century placed power and politics and the poor in the center of theological concern, and the critical school associated with figures like Johann Baptist Metz jolted many Christians out of complacent cultural accommodation.[10] But the figure more than any other who has sparked a recovery of the roots of political theology is the Anglican moral theologian Oliver O'Donovan.

Presently professor of Christian ethics and practical theology at the University of Edinburgh, Oliver O'Donovan over the course of some two decades of scholarly work has given intense scrutiny to the question of authority, politics, and judgment. Authority occupies the central part of his first major work, *Resurrection and Moral Order*, where one finds treatments of authority and freedom, the authority of Christ, and the authority of the church.[11] If *Resurrection and Moral Order* is an

10 See Gustavo Gutiérrez, *A Theology of Liberation*, rev. ed. (Maryknoll, N.Y.: Orbis, 1988).

11 Oliver O'Donovan, *Resurrection and Moral Order* (Leicester, England: Inter-Varsity Press, and Grand Rapids, Mich.: Eerdmans, 1986). There is a second edition, unchanged except for the addition of a "Prologue" (Leicester, England: Apollos, and Grand Rapids, Mich.: Eerdmans, 1994). Citations to page numbers are the same in either edition.

"outline" of evangelical ethics, *The Desire of the Nations*, O'Donovan's second broad-scale work, is an "outline" of political theology.[12] Here O'Donovan has an intensive analysis of political authority in particular, a project which he continues in *The Ways of Judgment*, his third and latest major work.[13] O'Donovan's project has not gone uncriticized. Nonetheless, it has been broadly recognized as a masterful rediscovery of political theology in the sense of theological reflection upon our governed life together. It will long be the reference point for future theological discussion of political authority.[14] Here I will approach O'Donovan's understanding of political authority by first sketching his understanding of authority in general.

Like Hannah Arendt, O'Donovan distinguishes authority from persuasion, on the one hand, and from coercion, on the other.[15] Coercion by itself is the imposition of will to the diminishment or destruction of free human action, inasmuch as it operates by taking away the agency of the persons upon whom it is imposed, turning them into passive beings. Authority, by contrast, is what makes action truly human. Yet authority is not merely a reasonable argument. Authority points to a good, but it does not do so by persuasion. Authority takes us beyond what reason alone would yield—and in this O'Donovan is in agreement with what we have seen before. But what we have in an authority, nonetheless, is not an absence of reasons. That is to say, authority may go beyond reason, yet it retains its own distinctive intelligibility.

The intelligibility of authority has three grounds. First, authority should be understood in terms of natural goods—such things as beauty, age and community (tradition), might, and wisdom—which

12 Oliver O'Donovan, *The Desire of the Nations* (Cambridge: University of Cambridge Press, 1996).

13 Oliver O'Donovan, *The Ways of Judgment* (Grand Rapids, Mich.: Eerdmans, 2005). In addition to these three seminal books, O'Donovan and his wife, Joan Lockwood O'Donovan, have published numerous articles on topics and figures in political theology. For a selection, see *Bonds of Imperfection* (Grand Rapids, Mich.: Eerdmans, 2004). They also edited the valuable collection, *From Irenaeus to Grotius: A Sourcebook in Christian Political Thought* (Grand Rapids, Mich.: Eerdmans, 1999).

14 An extensive symposium on *The Desire of the Nations* is in *Studies in Christian Ethics* 11.2 (1998), 1–110. See also Craig Bartholomew et al., ed., *A Royal Priesthood? The Use of the Bible Ethically and Politically: A Dialogue with Oliver O'Donovan* (Carlisle, Cumbria, U.K.: Paternoster, and Grand Rapids, Mich.: Zondervan, 2002).

15 For Hannah Arendt, see her "What Is Authority?" in *Between Past and Future*, new ed. (New York: Viking Press, 1968), 91–141; here, 92–3. For O'Donovan, see *The Desire of the Nations*, 30–1. Similar schemata are sketched by Stephen Sykes in his *Power and Christian Theology* (London: Continuum, 2006), 9.

are sufficient grounds for free action. These goods, while not themselves authorities, can (when mediated to us by persons who have authority) command or compel free human response by virtue simply of themselves. Authority is rooted in them; authority is thus "what we encounter in the world which makes it meaningful to act."[16] So does O'Donovan root authority broadly, in nature and in human anthropology. This corresponds to what we have been calling social authority, and it reminds us again of the paradox of human free action.

But natural goods are not the only intelligible ground of authority. O'Donovan goes on to identify what he calls the authority of truth itself. Truth also grounds authority, and it does so continually; but it calls for authoritative determination particularly in situations where natural goods conflict with each other, or when the perpetuation of what has hitherto been a good brings about an injustice. For instance, beauty, a natural good, summons us to preserve a hillside underneath which, however, lies a metal of industrial importance whose extraction, thus, is also summoned by a natural good, in this case the good of might. The determination of which competing good is truly authoritative is what we mean by the authority of truth, which is also called moral authority. It is found when an authority (person or persons) subjects the claims of created goods "to the review of a higher authority," namely, the authority of the truth of "the world as an ordered whole," in the light of which may be discerned "the good of human action which conforms to the truth of the created order."[17] Moral authority, we may say, is an aspect of what we have seen before in our consideration of epistemic authority. The seeker who would have epistemic authority strives to discern how the world really is—in O'Donovan's terms, how the natural goods truly fit together in the case at hand.

Finally, O'Donovan identifies a third ground for the intelligibility of authority. In *Resurrection and Moral Order* he calls it the authority of "injured right." This ground of authority cries forth for justice to be enacted. The emphasis is not on the adjective "injured," but on the dynamism of justice. This third ground of authority lies in the

16 O'Donovan, *Resurrection and Moral Order*, 122. See also O'Donovan, *The Ways of Judgment*, 131–2, where O'Donovan corrects his earlier identification of natural goods as authorities themselves. The "key difference about authority...is that the ground of action is not immediate, but mediated through another agent." It is in appreciation of this point that I have insisted throughout this book that authority is personal.

17 *Resurrection and Moral Order*, 125.

performative concept of "right"; it is the authority that is "commanded" by those who engage in promoting right, i.e., justice.[18]

Natural good, truth, and the enactment of right ground authority, and thus the commands of authority and the obedience it summons forth take us beyond that of which we could be persuaded by reason, without however losing thereby an inherent intelligibility. That is why authority is neither mere persuasion nor brute force. Authority neither imposes upon nor restricts human freedom, but is rather that which gives a point to free action.

And in doing so, the exercise of authority is capable of bringing about something like awe. This is a significant moment, the recognition by the people that an authority is taking them to a good that is truly theirs but would not, without authority, have been within their grasp or perhaps even their sight. So an orchestra may be surprised and, in a sense, swept away by their own performance of a new work that their conductor had urged upon them. Or a judge may discover unexpected yet illuminating parallels to a contemporary problem in a dusty and forgotten case. Or a crime victim may find that the perspicacious judgment of the court has strangely liberated her future life from the fault committed against her.

Now the reception of authority is not part of its ground; social, epistemic, and political authority do not become so on account of their being received. And of course, the recognition of authority need not be a moment of praise. A performer may never enjoy the Hindemith but nonetheless see the conductor's authority. An expert's determination of a problem's solution may be admitted as authoritative without being understood from the inside. But most commonly of all, government's actions may feel restrictive. I may never enjoy paying my taxes while nevertheless recognizing that the government that commands me to do so is my government. All this being granted, there yet remain occasions of the exercise of authority that *are* received with thanks by those whom authority commands—received with thanks, even praise, even a bit of awe. These are moments that approach worship, moments of gratitude for the good, the truth, the right that authority has commanded.

18 *Resurrection and Moral Order*, 124. In *The Ways of Judgment*, 143, O'Donovan says his earlier use of "injured" can be misleading, since the "sense of 'right' in question is the *enactment* of right, and authority is commanded by all active resistance to wrong" (emphasis original).

Herein, of course, is a danger. For authorities are persons and not gods to be worshiped. They do command obedience, but they cannot command the obedience of worship. "Those who present us with something we must do impose responsibility on us as well as freedom."[19] Yet this responsibility that they lay upon us, and which always comes to us in a particular, is not a responsibility to the authority itself, but to that which authority conveys.

For true authority is necessarily self-effacing: it points beyond itself to its point, the truth, the good, the right it is enacting and to which it is summoning us.[20] And as we noted in Chapter 2, no human authority can be self-standing. The centurion has authority because he is under authority; and Jesus likewise, because he is under authority, has authority. At the same time that authority lays responsibility upon a person it also authorizes or enables him freely to issue effective commands. Authority, "the objective correlate of freedom," essentially embeds itself in a social web of interrelationships.[21]

What then is the distinctive character of political authority? O'Donovan shows us that it is a particular mediation in society by which goods of creation, truth, and right lay their claim upon us. It is not the only way they do so; in any society there will be multiple organizations of various sorts—such as musical associations, service clubs, educational institutions, what I have called sometimes "mini-societies"—each of which, although lacking the power of the state, still is a means of some good claiming us for free and responsible action.[22]

19 *The Ways of Judgment*, 133.

20 O'Donovan suggests that to grasp this point we think of the difference between tradition and traditionalism, or between the strength of wisdom and that of technocracy. Christian tradition points beyond itself to the truth of Christ; traditionalism points only to itself. Wisdom which derives from the truth about how things are points to that truth; technocracy points to itself as its own authority. *Resurrection and Moral Order*, 126.

21 O'Donovan has defined authority as "the objective correlate of freedom": *Resurrection and Moral Order*, 122; *The Desire of the Nations*, 30. In his as yet unpublished 2009 Birks Lectures at McGill University, O'Donovan finds a looseness in this formulation and proposes to describe authority as "an event in which reality is communicated to practical reason." This revised formulation rightly emphasizes authority as a performative concept, and does not retreat from authority being the objective correlate of freedom, its performances being "disclosures of reality that we mediate to one another" by which we are enabled to act freely.

22 "[T]here is a multitude of non-political authorities, constituted by the ordinary relations of society, which direct us to perform certain actions: doctors, teachers, parents, employers.... In these relations, where two parties are not equally capable of envisaging the goods of action, one is dependent upon the direction of the other." *The Ways of Judgment*, 130.

Nonetheless, one could not have a society as a whole without political authority: for that authority is the objective correlate to the freedom of the society as such.[23] As O'Donovan remarks, the only examples we have of depoliticized societies are those in crisis or decay (e.g., Somalia in the 1990s).

We can say more about the nature of political authority. Through a careful study that begins with God's political authority as the ruler of Israel in the Old Testament, O'Donovan identifies three elements that are conjoined in political authority. Each element is necessary, and their effective combination in one agency is also necessary. O'Donovan puts the point in the form of a theorem: "*Political authority arises where power, the execution of right and the perpetuation of tradition are assured together in one coordinated agency.*"[24] Now the three elements could be known by different names. For "power" one might say "salvation" or "the ability to defeat one's enemies." For "the execution of right" one might say "justice" or "judgment." For "the perpetuation of tradition" one might say "law" or "the safeguarding of communal identity." Still, O'Donovan insists, by whatever names they are called, these three elements—power, right, and tradition—must be present for there to be true political authority.

By contrast, the forms of authority that we have previously considered lack some of these three elements and lack, thereby, the fullness of concern for the community as a whole that political authority carries. Social authority, for instance, might bear principally upon the third element only (perpetuation of tradition), which is in effect the mediation of natural good for a particular people at a particular time. It is good, for instance, that there be orchestras in order that Mozart's symphonic works not be forgotten or lost; good, also, that orchestras perform new works that carry forth the musical tradition in creative freshness. In order to justify the existence of a symphonic orchestra, one need point to nothing else than this created good. One can imagine other forms of social authority that would bear principally upon

23 See *The Desire of the Nations*, 30ff.

24 *The Desire of the Nations*, 46; emphasis original. In an earlier discussion of political authority, O'Donovan had used the terms "might," "tradition," and "injured right," the first two being natural authorities, as stated above. In 1994 he wrote that he now preferred "power" to "might," in order (I presume) to distinguish it from "force." See *Resurrection and Moral Order*, 128, and then "Prologue to the second edition," xx. Another change of emphasis is that in *The Desire of the Nations* O'Donovan is concerned to emphasize the dynamism of "right"—that judgment is a performative concept, something done, an activity and not a possession.

the second element only (execution of right), addressing themselves to the correction of injustices by means that do not involve political power. One might think of certain charitable organizations or trade unions in this regard. Epistemic authority, too, seems to bear upon the second element, insofar as it is directed to the solution of problems, the discovery of the truth about how things really are. But when the concern for the perpetuation of the tradition of a people marries the enactment of judgment and bears the power to achieve those ends, then we have authority that is distinctively political.

O'Donovan achieves this understanding of political authority by means of careful exegetical work, first and primarily in the Old Testament, but carried through the New and then traced through Christian tradition.[25] God revealed that he was king of Israel by his might in protecting Israel from its enemies, by his granting of judgment, and by his protection of the people's identity, principally by giving them the Law but also by giving them a land of their own. Jesus' kingship too shows these three elements: he has power over disease and demons (and ultimately over death); his teaching and his life as a whole is a definitive judgment upon sin and the forward-looking enactment of a new situation given precisely through that judgment; and by an authoritative, decisive interpretation of the Law, Jesus draws forth a new people who recognize his voice as the liberating voice of truth.

If we follow O'Donovan and understand political authority as that which is held by a personal agency in which power, judgment, and tradition are united, then the coming of Christ requires us to make a fundamental distinction, namely, between political authority itself, and political authority as it exists today, i.e., after the coming of Christ. And this distinction has profound ramifications for our understanding of our subject, as we will see.

The Christian claim that God the Father vindicated his Son by raising him from the dead and exalting him to his "right hand" is the claim that the Son has come into his kingdom. Seated, as the familiar line of the Christian creed has it, "at the right hand of the Father," he rules the universe. By Christian doctrine, then, all earthly rulers have been superseded by Christ, who now possesses the fullness of political authority. Christ has won a powerful victory for his people, a people he is drawing out from all nations by securing for them an identity and providing for them ever-flowing justice.

25 See *The Desire of the Nations*, chapters 2–4 for the exegetical work, chapters 5–6 for the historical.

This doctrine of Christ's full political authority, implicit and explicit in the understanding of the ascension and "session" of Christ,[26] changes the character of earthly political authority. No longer need earthly rulers be concerned about the first element of political authority, "salvation" or military victory or survival. Survival, mere extension in time, can no longer be the point of Rome or the United States or any other political society. Self-defense cannot justify Christian political action any more than it can justify private action.[27] Similarly, political authority is no longer concerned with the creation of law or, in general, with the preservation of social identity. Law has been decisively promulgated by Christ and ratified in his exaltation; the social identity that matters is found in his kingdom. What remains in this temporal period between Christ's ascension and his ultimate return—a period Christians learned to call "secular," meaning "pertaining to this age (only)"—is the second element of political authority, the provision of judgment. This was intuited early, as for instance in Romans 13 where Paul ascribes the punishment of vice and the promotion of good as the legitimate functions of secular government. The alternative, figured for instance in Revelation 13, is "empire": the idolatrous presumption

26 In this regard, see in general Douglas Farrow, *Ascension and Ecclesia: On the Significance of the Doctrine of the Ascension for Ecclesiology and Christian Cosmology* (Grand Rapids, Mich.: Eerdmans, 1999), and in particular Douglas Farrow, "Confessing Christ Coming," in Christopher R. Seitz, ed., *Nicene Christianity* (Grand Rapids, Mich.: Brazos Press, 2001), 133–48.

27 Which is why Augustine grounded justifiable war—only—on the defense of an innocent neighbor from wrongful attack, remembering, of course, that the enemy also remains a neighbor. See Paul Ramsey, "The Just War According to Saint Augustine," in his *War and the Christian Conscience* (Durham, N.C.: Duke University Press, 1961), 15–33. See also Paul Ramsey, *The Just War* (New York: Charles Scribner's Sons, 1968), 150–1.

The *locus classicus* for the discussion of the justifiability of killing in self-defense is Aquinas, *Summa theologiae*, II-II, q. 64, a. 7, wherein is introduced the point that an action can have two effects, one intended and the other "beside" the intention. However one interprets Aquinas's argument—and it is hardly a full-blown "principle of double-effect"—it is clearly a development from earlier tradition that forbade Christians from killing in self-defense. See Kevin L. Flannery, *Acts Amid Precepts* (Washington, D.C.: Catholic University of America Press, 2001), chapter 7. See also T. A. Cavanaugh, *Double-Effect Reasoning: Doing Good and Avoiding Evil* (Oxford: Clarendon Press, 2006), especially chapter 1. For an interpretation of the so-called principle of double effect as illuminating "a quite specific truth about murder" while not providing "a formal truth about the shape of the human act as such," see O'Donovan, *Resurrection and Moral Order*, 191–4. And on this point generally, see O'Donovan, *The Ways of Judgment*, 208–10.

of government to provide power and identity, thereby refusing to be merely secular, rising up in defiance of that which has been done already in Christ.[28]

So the Christian insight into political authority is that all the functions of government can be, and should be, re-conceived as the exercise of judgment. The illustration earlier in this chapter attempted to foreshadow this conclusion. Judgment is bidirectional, a moment which brings the past to a head while simultaneously laying the conditions for the future. It is not only what courts do, but legislatures and executives also provide judgment. Its conditions, we should specify, are the limitations imposed by this present theological age, now some 2000 years in length; the age known as "secular." Judgment is given by a political authority who is, also, under authority. Ultimate judgment is given by no court, but only by God. Secular judgment, and thus secular political authority, is provisional and circumscribed. It must act within finite time and with less than comprehensive information, and thus sometimes will err. But the fear of error cannot freeze its acting; without judgment, without the exercise of political authority, the good which judgment provides will not be had, and society will sink into a depoliticized morass.

To conclude this section, we should return to the crucial question of power to see if we have achieved a better understanding of it. In a broad sense, "power" refers to the ability to get things done. So in that sense power is an element of all authority, including social and epistemic authority that we have looked at in earlier chapters. Power belongs particularly to political authority, however; and here it can entail the use of coercive force. Political authority involves the power of government to command and, if the command is not obeyed, to compel and (if necessary) to punish. We may imagine that in a world without sin government would never need to compel obedience, because all the commands of political authority would be obeyed freely by every citizen. And so it seems to me that the coercive quality of political power belongs to this world only. Secular political authority may and sometimes must be coercive; but in the kingdom of heaven there is no coercion. Yet did we not, earlier in this chapter, distinguish authority as a species of power from the power that is merely coercive force? Indeed,

28 For this paragraph generally, see *The Desire of the Nations*, 146–57. The typological contrast of Romans 13 and Revelation 13 is made by, among others, Helmut Thielicke in *Theological Ethics*, vol. 2, *Politics* (Grand Rapids, Mich.: Eerdmans, 1979 [repr. of 1969 ed.]); see especially chapters 2 and 5.

it is the distinctiveness of political authority, lying between mere reason and dumb coercion, that compels our sense that a sort of failure has occurred whenever government must forcibly compel action. Nonetheless, it is significant to note, yet again, that in fact political authority's commands are obeyed for the most part, even in this world of sin, without that authority needing to resort to force. The threat of fines and imprisonments is enough for most of us, most of the time, to stay within the bounds prescribed by political authority. And perhaps even that way of putting it is overly drear. Perhaps there is something of worth in political authority itself, our intuitive grasp that it conveys a good to us that otherwise we would not have had, that inclines us to render obedience to its commands. Political authority is an on-going provision of justice, a performance of right, a continuing demarcation of a line between right and wrong, that is essential to our living together as human beings. And if we cannot live together, then we will not be able to be human. In recognition of such truths as these, we acknowledge political authority, thereby, as O'Donovan says, proving our political identity.[29]

Yet the fact that political authority entails power—coercive power, in such circumstances as are marked by sin, i.e., any earthly circumstances this side of the return of Christ—means that the problem of error is even more critical in political authority than it is in other forms of authority. For political authority can err, and when it does err, it cannot give back what it has taken. The person wrongly convicted of a heinous crime and subjected to capital punishment: his life cannot be returned. The prisoner wrongly committed to jail: her years of incarceration are lost. True, a financial penalty can be returned with interest, and sometimes a wrong in punishment can be compensated for by a financial award. Nonetheless, time in the human universe flows only in one direction, and the loss of time—the loss of a part of one's life—can never be returned. I will address, in Chapter 6, the general problem of authority and error, and at that time will ask what the proper means are for disputing authority. For now let us note, first,

29 He puts it as a theorem: "*In acknowledging political authority, society proves its political identity.*" In Israel's case, to acknowledge God's kingship was to give praise of the Lord; see the many psalmic cries of the sort, "The Lord is king; let the earth rejoice." For the Christian, Christ's political authority is acknowledged by faith, by which Christians prove their political identity. But the theorem is true for all political authority and gives insight into secular politics. *The Desire of the Nations*, 47; emphasis original.

that when authority is understood to be self-effacing by O'Donovan, it is so because it has an intelligibility about it, albeit not the fullness of the intelligibility of persuasive reason. There is here a correspondence between O'Donovan's thought and Polanyi's explication of a tacit element of knowledge that goes beyond anything that can be said. When authority is self-effacing, it cannot bear the arbitrariness that points to authority itself as the reason for acting. Furthermore, as Polanyi reckoned with the possibility (and oft reality) that authorities could be wrong, so O'Donovan holds that political authorities can fail to provide justice or to maintain tradition. What happens then? There can be, O'Donovan says, an unofficial element in society itself that carries society's traditions through a period of crisis. In the Israel of the Old Testament, this happened in the prophetic movements that arose in the time of the injustice and apostasy of kings. Characteristically, O'Donovan expresses this situation in the form of a theorem: "*the conscience of the individual members of a community is a repository of the moral understanding which shaped it, and may serve to perpetuate it in a crisis of collapsing morale or institution.*"[30] Individual conscience may become an ark of sorts, to carry judgment and tradition through a period of ineffective or corrupt government.

The Public, the Political, and Certainty

Let me raise three objections to the account of political authority given in the previous section. In replying to these objections, I will make explicit the difference between "the public" and "the political," which are both to be distinguished from "the private." This distinction, in turn, will shed more light on the forms of authority discussed earlier, and allow a sharper focus to be placed on the question of certainty.

Objection 1. Political authority concerns itself with the good of the society as a whole. But with its monopoly on coercive force, political authority will be tempted to arrogate unto itself the entire public realm. What is there, in this account, to keep political authority from becoming totalitarian?

Objection 2. It seems there is confusion between social and political authority. In Chapter 2 on social authority, the argument was made

30 *The Desire of the Nations*, 80; emphasis original.

for its necessity on the grounds that there had to be an agency to will the common good materially. But is not that agency, simply, political authority? And if so, then the necessity for having a distinctive form of authority called "political" disappears.

Objection 3. How can political authority know what to do? That is to say, in the particulars of a given situation, how does political authority work? It seems that political authority requires expert knowledge. But the argument of Chapter 3 has shown us that expert knowledge is the achievement of epistemic authority. So political authority does not seem to be different from epistemic authority.

Reply to objection 1. The first objection will resonate strongly with the anti-authority instincts of contemporary western society. We distrust those who have power, and we interpret exercises of power through the hermeneutics of suspicion. Namely, we suspect that political authorities will ever seek to increase the power at their disposal, and will try to do so without regard for the common good. The end of that trajectory is rightly labeled "totalitarian," for the totalitarian state is one that has obliterated any competing centers of authority, leaving the individual naked before the state without such mediating institutions as churches, labor unions, or voluntary associations (the "mini-societies" as this book has often called them). How indeed does the account of political authority, given earlier in this chapter, avoid the totalitarian trajectory?

It does so in at least two ways. First, there is the analysis that political authority can be distinguished from sheer coercion by its inherent intelligibility. Political authority is grounded in natural goods (as is social authority) and in truth (as is epistemic authority), but it is particularly grounded in "right," the activity of making the judgments between right and wrong that are necessary for a political community. Political authority can point to what it is about, the securing of these goods, and it can be recognized as doing so. By contrast, totalitarianism, or any attempt to accumulate power for its own sake, points to no good beyond itself. That is to say, totalitarianism has no intelligibility beyond its own self-preservation. Second, there is the nested character of all human authority, that to have it is to be under it. In the case of political authority in the secular era following the ascension of Christ, its nested character means that it has authority of judgment only. Someone else has the fullness of political authority, and he rules over, and will be the ultimate judge of, secular political authorities. By contrast, totalitarianism is an implicit rejection of the limits imposed by this secular age. The Christian tradition of political thought will see totalitarian regimes as rebellious and implicitly idolatrous.

Thus political authority, as understood in this chapter, is limited by its need to possess its characteristic form of intelligibility, and it is limited in its scope to something less than the fullness of political authority as exercised by the ascended Christ. Both forms of limitation point to the helpful distinction between the political realm and the public realm. In fact, there is a three-way distinction to be made, if we follow O'Donovan's lead in cutting through terminology that is often confusing. It is a distinction among the different ways that human activity relates to human society. The *political*, he offers, refers to reflexive defense of the common good. The *public*, differing from the political, pursues the common good directly. And the *private*, in distinction from both the political and the public, engages the common good indirectly.[31] This three-way distinction coheres with our earlier discussions not only of political authority but of social authority. Simon taught us that the common good requires that particular goods be willed materially by individuals: this is the indirect engagement of the common good by the private realm. Mini-societies, such as orchestras and neighborhood associations, may work to advance certain goods or to mitigate situations where the good is absent or diminished: this is the direct engagement of the common good by the public realm. But government secures what society needs by securing right judgment, the activity that by looking at once backward and forward defends and preserves the common good reflexively.

So this three-fold distinction that makes political activity defensive and reflexive—not the sole custodian of the common good, and one whose actions come in response to given situations—is another feature, built into this analysis of political authority, which shows the great gap between political authority and totalitarianism. But it also cautions us against identifying political authority with "the good of society as a whole," full stop. Political authority's concern, yes, is with the common good, and thus the good of society as a whole, but it is a responsive concern, which is what we mean when we say it is defensive and reflexive.[32] Other agencies, whose place is squarely in the public realm, are also concerned with the common good. And even the private realm contains agencies which, while promoting

31 See *The Ways of Judgment*, 55–7.

32 See O'Donovan's discussion of government as responsible: *The Desire of the Nations*, 231–4.

particular goods (such as, to pick up on Simon's early example, the study of Latin), by that very activity promote the common good, but do so indirectly.

Reply to objection 2. The distinction of the political, the public, and the private helps address the second objection, which asks if the function of authority identified by Simon as most essential, namely the function of willing the common good materially, which this book placed in Chapter 2 under social authority, is not itself simply political authority. If we accept the distinction of the political and the public, then it would seem that to will the common good materially, if that is done in a direct manner, could be done by a non-political social authority. For the function of political authority is defensive: it wills the common good materially, indeed; the adverb "materially" points to the conjunction of power, judgment, and law. But we may conceive large-scale non-governmental "public" enterprises which summon our free assent and yet are able to function without the use of coercive force. In a close-knit community, such an enterprise might be a neighborhood association, even an unincorporated and largely informal neighborhood association, whose manifest applicability to the common good would draw forth near-universal consent and cooperation. It is harder to imagine such enterprises in larger and diverse communities, although perhaps such charitable organizations as the International Red Cross may serve as suggestive illustrations.

The objection provides the opportunity to harmonize some of the terms of discussion up to this point, and make explicit a number of implicit interconnections. "Society" I take to be a highly general term referring to a group of persons somehow held or brought together. Individuals may belong to many such societies, which can overlap and be of wider or narrower, or higher or lower, extent. Within some societies, particularly those on a wide or high level, there will be political authority. Smaller societies will exist within larger ones that have political authority, and some political authorities will be under other, wider and higher, authorities. Within a society that includes political authority, there will be political, public, and private agencies. Social authority is exercised by the latter two: public and private agencies. Political authority is reserved to political agencies.

Reply to objection 3. The third objection concerns the relationship of political and epistemic authority. This is not so neatly handled as the relationship of political and social authority, because there is no spatial metaphor of "wider" and "higher" that can be used to link the two. But we can link some of O'Donovan's epistemological claims with the account of epistemic authority drawn from Polanyi in the previous chapter.

Polanyi emphasizes truth as the external anchor of our personal knowledge. Although we can never be sure that a decision we have reached will stand under the scrutiny of others, nonetheless we venture that decision with an assurance that is not willful but a faithful response to the intellectual passion that drives us to know the truth. O'Donovan should find this conclusion congenial, although I would expect him to attain it in evangelical mode through a reading of the Scriptures.[33] It is a key element of O'Donovan's anthropology that human reason is never able to achieve self-transcendence. And therefore all the conclusions of our reason stand under the eschatological judgment of God, who alone will vindicate nature and history at the end of time.[34] Yet, as Polanyi insisted that the personal character of all knowledge does not entail relativism or subjectivism, so O'Donovan insists that we do have access to truth, as a gift of the Holy Spirit.

This is an anthropological conclusion, true for people in general and thus true in particular for people who bear political authority. Hence, it seems to me, we may think of political authorities as a certain kind of epistemic authorities. Their function is to articulate judgment which, necessarily, they must promulgate as definitive judgment, just as an epistemic authority (of any kind) must assert her conclusions without reservation. There is no probable judgment in political judgment, any more than an epistemic authority may assert her conclusions probabilistically.

How does a political authority know what to do? The question entails the same paradoxical circularity as epistemic authority in general. To learn how to will the common good materially, that is (to be specific about political authority) to learn how to make good judgments at the right time and in the right way: that would require apprenticeship, a trusting of persons who are seen to have true political authority, and then the perfection of expertise, but always within a system of interlocking authorities. One grows in politics just as one grows in

33 I am not aware of O'Donovan having commented upon Polanyi in his published work. In a letter he once indicated that Polanyi had been a figure on the horizon of his thought, but he offered no judgment upon him.

34 Therefore O'Donovan has reservations about any natural law theory, despite "strong sympathy" with its "more realist versions." For how could reason ever give us a premise that is epistemologically certain, upon which conscience would then operate and draw conclusions? See *Resurrection and Moral Order*, 85–7.

carpentry, industrial management, or music, always, however, with the distinction that in politics one wields the potentially coercive power of government. The claim that an authority makes (any person in authority, including political authority) is that she points truthfully to a good. Of course, she may fail to do so. Which means that, in addition to the first objection that concerned willful power-seeking as a perversion of political authority, we can add stupidity. Authorities may fail by being clueless as much as by being wicked.

Christ the King and Earthly Rulers

Before concluding this chapter it is necessary to indicate something that political theology does *not* say.

A quick assumption not infrequently made is that anyone who speaks theologically about political authority has an agenda, secret or otherwise, to impose theocratic rule upon society. Such persons are often assumed, in particular, to long for the return of some form of Christendom. The analysis of this chapter shows already the erroneousness of that assumption. According to the Christian reflection upon political authority given above, the exercise of political authority is understood to stand under the ultimate judgment of Christ, and to be circumscribed in its exercise by the conditions imposed by the present secular age (the age, as said above, that follows upon Christ's ascension). From the understanding of political authority as thus secular there follows no necessity that it be exercised by persons with sacerdotal powers, nor by persons appointed by the church, nor indeed by persons who make explicit recognition of the authority of Christ.

This conclusion will be clearer, however, if we take stock of what we mean when we speak of Christendom.[35] The term "Christendom" refers to a historical period, principally in Europe, within which those who exercised political authority were expected to understand themselves as being under the authority of Christ the King. Political authority professed Christ while being secular. Symbolically, the period may be understood as beginning with the Edict of Milan in 313, whereby Christianity became a tolerated religion of the Roman Empire. Our present situation is widely acknowledged as one of "post-Christendom,"

35 Here again I give the gist of an account more fully developed by O'Donovan. See *The Desire of the Nations*, 245–6.

but it is harder to pick a symbolic concluding date. O'Donovan offers as one candidate, doubtless with British irony, the year 1791 in which the First Amendment to the United States Constitution was adopted.

So Christendom had a long run. It was dominated by the question of the relation of religious and secular authority, but there was no single dominant answer to that question. That is to say, Christendom was not necessarily theocratic. At times in Christendom, the religious and secular authorities were understood as parallel, at other times one subservient to the other (and it could be either one subservient to either). At yet other times there was frustration at the old struggles and an attempt to find some other authority that supervened over them both (one candidate was the authority of the Word). What was constant, however, was the expectation that political authority recognized the higher, and also political, authority of Christ ascended and seated at the right hand of the Father.

It is important to be clear that there is no intrinsic argument in political theology either for or against the idea of Christendom. There are many obvious (so they will seem to us) pragmatic arguments against Christendom. We are aware of how the church tends to be corrupted when it has political influence. We are aware, also, of the superficiality that easily attends public pronouncements of religious faith. But pragmatic arguments a principle do not make.

Christian proclamation of the kingship of Christ does not stand or fall upon the basis of whether the secular political order acknowledges that kingship. But here is the key point: true Christian proclamation is necessarily catholic in its extent. There is no person whom the Gospel does not address. *This includes persons who have political authority.* So we might put it slightly ironically. The faithful church will address the message of the kingship of Christ even to those who are kings, even though it knows that if the proclamation meets with acceptance the church can anticipate manifold future problems, particularly the problems of the purity of the church's witness and the sincerity of civil religion.

In other words, something like Christendom, far from being the point of the church's witness, might better be understood as an unavoidable risk of that witness. St. Paul wrote poetically of every knee bending before and every tongue confessing the name of Jesus (Phil. 2.10–11). If the church's mission meets with success, there could well result a political society so permeated with Christian understanding that its political authorities could acknowledge the higher political rule of Christ without thereby becoming coercive of others' beliefs.[36] To foreclose that possibility, as seemingly has been done with the First Amendment, cannot be understood as fidelity to the Christian message.[37]

36 In the Vatican II declaration on religion freedom there is a carefully-worded acknowledgment that, in limited yet not unimaginable conditions, there could be an established church without that establishment being coercive against the religious freedom that rightly belongs to each human person. See *Dignitatis humanae*, sec. 6; in Walter M. Abbott, ed., *The Documents of Vatican II* (New York: Guild Press, 1966). In the same volume, see also note 17 on page 685 by John Courtney Murray. I would argue that, in a predominantly Christian society, it would be possible to have both an established church and religious freedom. What would be coercive would be measures such as religious tests for public office and the like. And what must also be acknowledged is that establishment can have no intrinsic permanency; if the character of society changed, so should this character of its political order.

37 I speak here of the First Amendment as it has been interpreted judicially. On its own terms, the First Amendment requires only that there be no national established church; it does not attempt a separation of church and state. Disestablishment is compatible with Christendom, as it is compatible with the bearers of political authority still acknowledging the kingship of Christ. For an account of how the First Amendment when adopted did not entail separation, and how it came to be taken as doing so, see the masterful work of Philip Hamburger, *Separation of Church and State* (Cambridge, Mass.: Harvard University Press, 2002).

Chapter 5

AUTHORITY AND GOD: ECCLESIAL AUTHORITY

The Odd Place of the Church in this Discussion

This examination of authority has been undertaken so far from a human point of view. To succeed at being a human, I have urged, is to be able to live together with others. Upon examination, it turns out that to live together with others in any sort of society requires that authority be there. And to live together with the skills of knowing and discerning the truth about the world, that also requires the existence of authority. Thus, to be human at all requires authority both social and epistemic. Furthermore, when we consider social authority at its most extensive—the authority that governs a society—we encounter political authority, a species that is social and epistemic but also has coercive force at its disposal.

But none of this discussion has been carried on with theological blinders. Early on, the biblical understanding of authority confirmed our sense that it is a complex, structured affair; that to be a person "in authority" or to "have authority" is not to be pushed up to the top of a pyramid, but rather to be one who is also *under* authority. Then the relationship of authority and truth, which Michael Polanyi helped us see as a necessarily dialectical one in which authority points beyond itself to truth and, at the same time, the truth as apprehended raises a question upon authority, was itself a dialectical relationship expressed by Jesus when he said, as one with authority, that his mission was to bring knowledge of the truth, which knowledge in turn would be liberating. Likewise in our study of authority and power, theology was present when we turned back to the roots of political theology, as exposed by Oliver O'Donovan, where we could see the nature of political authority.

This chapter does not form a simple progression with the three chapters that have preceded it, and that is because to move from social, epistemic, and political authority to ecclesial authority is not to move to yet another field or dimension of human existence. For the church is not rightly understood as another society, alongside, say, the symphony and the academy, existing in conjunction with them in a common political society. To make the church out to be another mini-society or voluntary association is to reject its claims of bearing revealed and transcendent truth. Nor is the church "over" society, as a super-City within which not only the symphony and the university but also every political society also exists. To make the church out to be the universal political society is to deny in some fundamental way both the autonomous and natural importance of human political societies and, also, the provisionality of the church itself as a witness to a kingdom that is in important ways still to come.

Neither an association nor an epistemic allegiance, nor yet an overarching "umbrella" society, the church is a strange thing that fails to fit into any given categorical scheme.[1] Fortunately, we need not achieve the impossibility of mastering an unmasterable topic in order to learn from authority as we can see it in action in the church. Nor must the church as we experience it be healthy, faithful, and in general trouble-free. Even from an afflicted church we may learn something new about authority, and perhaps what we learn overall will be of some service to people in churches today who struggle with problems of authority.

By turning to "authority and God," this chapter will bring theology from the side to the center of our discussion. One might wonder how it is possible to bring God to the center. There is a simple answer, implicit indeed since our second chapter, and an answer which I fear is quite unenlightening. It is to say simply: God is the source of all authority. This is true, I am sure, but as a bare assertion it fails to illuminate. And it encourages unhelpful questions. For instance: If God is the source of all authority, then must we say he is the source of every

1 Which is why ecclesiology is a notoriously difficult subject. The brilliance of Avery Dulles's *Models of the Church* (expanded edition; New York: Doubleday, 1987) is not in the details of his various models, perceptive as those details are, but in his systematic accounting for the fact that no modeling of the church can be adequate. The church is in some sense an institution; it is also the body of Christ, and a sacrament, and a voice for justice and truth, and a servant, and a pilgrim community, and yet more. All these models have some truth, and yet each falls short of the reality.

decision made by current and past U.S. Presidents, or indeed by leaders of other nations, governors, mayors, and dog-catchers? In epistemic authority, do we see anything better if we claim God as the source of the authority of peer reviewers and the gatekeepers of the professions? In social authority, do we see anything new when we say every orchestra conductor has her authority from God?

Yet, located within the church, such questions can indeed turn out to be helpful. For the church is a place where the implications of God's being the source of all authority are somewhat clearer to our eyes, if not, alas, altogether lucid. The church is a *congregation* or a *synagogue*, words which speak etymologically of a "calling" or "bringing together." Those called together as church have come in some way to recognize God's authority. They are a congregation dedicated to the Truth (and here the capital letter impresses itself upon us). The church is not a political society and will never be one, but its mission is to point to one peculiar and ultimate political society: a kingdom of citizens who freely obey and follow their King, who live in a city of which their Lord is the light. As a society gathered for the sake of knowing the Truth and witnessing to God's kingdom, what can the church teach us about the relationship of God and authority?

Let us attend to another musical illustration.

Illustration: The Aria in Bach's *Saint Matthew Passion*

The *Saint Matthew Passion* of Johannes Sebastian Bach, a complex tapestry in sound, is not so much a concert-piece as a representation that holds before us the church called together—the church assembled. The proper shape of the assembled church is eucharistically determined, as it gathers in obedience to Jesus' command "Do this for the remembrance of me." But the most solemn gathering together ("congregation") of the church, since ancient times, has been to recall the extended narrative of the Passion. Within the event that is Bach's *Passion*,[2] the church comes together to attend to the saving events of Jesus' last supper, arrest, trial, suffering, crucifixion, death, and burial. In Bach's *Passion* these events are "recited" by solo voices who represent

2 For convenience I shall refer to the *Saint Matthew Passion* as, simply, the *Passion*; recognizing, of course, that Bach wrote other *Passion*s, which are not being considered here.

the main characters and the evangelist Matthew. At the beginning and at the end, and also at points interspersed throughout the story, Bach places his magnificent chorales, the large pieces sung by the chorus entire which, in singing them, gives voice to the congregation's own response to the story it is hearing. And along with the chorales are the parts considered by many people the most sublime of all, the arias. In each aria, an individual arises from the assembly and sings what amounts to a very personal confession of faith. The individual's aria does not advance the story-line of the *Passion,* nor is it the response of the church as a whole to the story. It is her—the individual's—response, her faithful acknowledgment, in the sight of all, that she owns for herself the sad deeds of Jesus' suffering and death.[3]

Let us look at the substance of these arias. The first one, *Buß' und Reu'* (section 10), follows upon the story of the woman who poured precious ointment on Jesus' head. Here an alto rises to confess that her own heart has been broken. She offers her tears as a precious balm for Jesus: "Guilt and pain / Break the sinful heart in twain, / So the teardrops of my weeping / A most soothing precious balm, / Beloved Jesus, doth offer thee."[4] By virtue of the aria, the singer identifies herself with a character in the sacred story, namely, the woman in the Passion who anointed Jesus. But to do so requires that the singer perform a leap across time: she must replace the precious ointment in the story with her own tears of sorrow in the present moment, tears she identifies as "a most soothing precious balm."

The faith expressed in such a leap of identification results in self-offering, as we see explicitly in the third aria when the soprano offers herself to Jesus. This self-oblation follows the recitation of the words of the Last Supper, *das ist mein Blut des neuen Testaments,* "this is my blood of the New Testament." The soprano rises first to confess, in a

3 When I speak here of the individual aria singer in the feminine gender, it is of course with an eye to contemporary performances, when the higher-voiced arias are sung by women; in what follows, I use "he" and "she" in rough correspondence to the pitch, yet with the over-arching image of the individual who rises from the congregation as feminine. It seems to me advantageous to speak often of the authorized individual as feminine, for many reasons, including but not limited to its corrective function upon our anthropological imagery, and the balance thereby given to the masculine language with which the Christian revelation normatively speaks of God. Nonetheless, it is all but certain that *all* the arias were sung by males in Bach's day, with the soprano arias taken by boys.

4 Text and translations herein are from the Choral Society of Durham, North Carolina, in *Matthäus Passion,* Saint Thomas Choir program (New York: Saint Thomas Church, 2009).

preparatory recitative, a mixture of grief and joy: "although my heart swims in tears because Jesus takes leave of us, yet his testament makes me glad." Immediately then she sings her aria, *Ich will dir mein Herze schenken* (section 19): "I will give my heart to thee; / Sink thyself in it, my Salvation. / I will submerge myself in thee." She offers herself to Jesus, at once asking him to come into her heart while pledging to enter into him. This mutual indwelling is common to eucharistic petitions (an Anglican will recall that the traditional "Prayer of Humble Access" concludes in its modern form with the request that "we may evermore dwell in him, and he in us"[5]). Through this aria, mutual indwelling is prayed for by the solo soprano voice.

Sometimes in Bach's *Passion* the chorus sings together in the first person, as in the chorale of section 21, *Erkenne mich, mein Hüter*: "Much good has befallen me. / My shepherd, take me to thee." Here we find the faith of the church called together, its members speaking in solidarity with each other for a common desire that is, at the same time, personal to each, that Jesus their shepherd would take each one to himself. But then arises again an individual, this time the tenor (section 26). Jesus is praying in the garden, asking his disciples to tarry and keep watch with him. It is a complex aria, for while the tenor professes fidelity, the chorus sings of its failure. *Ich will bei meinem Jesu wachen*, he says: "I will watch beside my Jesus," which the chorus counters with sad truth, *So schlafen unsre Sünden ein*: "Then our sins go to sleep."

In the aria of section 29, an individual professes he will gladly take up Jesus' cross and cup (*Gerne will ich mich bequemen*). Then an alto, in the sixth aria, section 36, laments Jesus' arrest and cries "Where has my Jesus gone?" Here the church by means of the chorus speaks words of assurance to her, that she will not be left alone: "Then we shall seek him with thee." In the next aria, section 41, the tenor says he will himself be patient under undeserved suffering. And so it continues, the individuals of the arias responding personally to the passion of Jesus, making their own lives contemporary with that narrative. When Peter weeps, the soloist prays God for mercy "for my tears' sake"; his sublime petition is that God see: "Heart and eyes weep before thee /

5 In the first Book of Common Prayer of 1548/49, the prayer concludes: "that we may continuallye dwell in hym, and he in us, that our synfull bodyes may bee made cleane by his body, and our soules washed through hys most precious bloud." Here the eucharistic mutual indwelling is prayed to be "continual," which we may see manifested in the petition of the soprano's aria that Jesus sink himself in her heart as she submerges (washes?) herself in him.

Bitterly" (section 47). When the chief priests refuse to take the money that Judas throws back at them, the aria is plaintive: "Give me back my Jesus" (section 51). When Pilate asks what evil Jesus has done, the solo soprano puts herself into the narrative: "He has done good to us all" (section 56). Her immediately following aria is her confession of faith: "Out of love my Saviour is willing to die, / Though he knows nothing of any sin, / So that eternal ruin / And the punishment of judgment / May not rest upon my soul." In the aria of section 61, the alto says that if her tears are not enough, "then take my heart away!" The bass asks Jesus to give his cross to him, and to help him carry it (section 66). The alto tells the congregation of the chorus that Jesus has his hand outstretched for us to grasp, so that we can find redemption in Jesus' arms (section 70).

In the final aria, *Mache dich, mein Herze, rein,* the bass sings: "Make thyself clean, my heart, / I will myself entomb Jesus" (section 75). The Passion narrative has reached its terminus, the entombment of Jesus in the grave owned by Joseph of Arimathea. But by means of the aria, a bass soloist has arisen as an individual Christian in the contemporary church to offer his own heart to be Jesus' tomb. "He shall henceforth in me / For ever and ever / Take his sweet rest." *Welt, geh aus, laß Jesum ein!* "World, begone, let Jesus in!" It is a turn of his own heart, away from the enticements of the "world" to the purity of the sacrificed Lord. And it is a recognition that there is not enough space in the heart for both to dwell at once.

What is happening when a soloist rises to sing an aria? The soloist is authorized by Bach to stand and sing; this is the plain truth of the text. In the performance, the soloist is authorized also by the conductor. But in that which the performance is about, the soloist speaks of her faith with authority. It is my view that Bach here gives us a model of the true functioning of authority in the church. The individual could not sing, as it were, authoritatively, were she not standing in the midst of the assembly of the faithful. The assembly of the faithful is the locus where we may find the exercise of authority. Yet the faithful, as a whole, only prepare the ground for the authority of the faithful individual who sings. The authority in the church as a whole is only potential and implicit; it is exercised—it comes alive—when the one stands to profess. Note too that what is said authoritatively is not the simple recitation of a scriptural text. Rather, it involves a leap that makes the sacred story contemporary to the singer. Often, what is said authoritatively entails an act of self-oblation. Again, the aria is sung with authority only because it is sung in the context of the sacred words. Thus, as there is no authority apart from the assembly, so is there no authority apart from Scripture. But Scripture alone, even when it is spoken in the midst of the assembly, is not where authority is being actualized. Nonetheless, authority is responsive. The soloist responds neither to Bach nor to the conductor; she speaks in the midst of the assembly but not to the assembly; she speaks in the context of the church's recitation of the salvific narrative but her words are not in the narrative. Her authority resides in the one in whom she is placing her faith. We have seen before that authority is always personal authority; here in the *Passion* we have a striking image of what that means.

Upon reflection, we may think it not surprising that Bach structured his *Passion* in this way. In the liturgy of the church, there is a similar instance in the baptism of an adult (and it is implicit in the baptism of a child). Presented for the sacrament by his sponsors, who represent the entire congregation of the faithful, the one being baptized stands to profess his faith in God. An old story about this was told to Augustine around the year 386, when Augustine was wavering and resisting the call of God to him, concerning Victorinus, an urbane "rhetor" of the city of Rome who was famous throughout the city and known to Augustine as a translator of Plotinus. When Victorinus himself finally confessed his desire to be baptized, the church officials offered to give him a private baptism—a concession that was perhaps pragmatic but certainly unwise. No, said Victorinus; I was not ashamed to profess error in public, why should I now fear to proclaim the truth before the people? And so, along with the others who were being baptized, he rose himself to a high place in the sight of the church assembly, through which had just run a great silence as the crowd began to realize who this man was who was stepping up to speak. Victorinus there declared his faith in the one God, Father, Son, and Holy Spirit; he proclaimed as well his trust in the one who had suffered his passion and endured his death for him.[6]

Authority in the church, then, appears as a sort of mysterious percolation. It requires that there be an assembly, and therefore it requires that there be the communal identity and structure that makes the assembly possible. To be specific, and to take a catholic ecclesiology as normative, authority requires that there be a given structure of ordained ministry, received creeds, and continually-renewed tradition. Above all, authority in the church requires the Scriptures,

6 Augustine, *Confessions* VIII.ii (3–5).

faithfully handed down and recited in the presence of all the faithful. But the odd thing we see in the church is that authority in the radical sense resides in none of those things: not in ordination, not in creed and tradition, not even in Scripture. Authority resides in the individual believer who, inspired by the Holy Spirit, proclaims faithfully her allegiance to the suffering Jesus, and thus to her Lord, and thus to the Triune Reality that is the source of all authority in heaven and earth.

Authority in the Church

The first paragraph of the first statement on authority that was to issue from the first Anglican-Roman Catholic International Commission (ARCIC) located authority with regard to the heart of the Christian faith:

> The confession of Christ as Lord is the heart of the Christian faith. To him God has given all authority in heaven and on earth. As Lord of the Church he bestows the Holy Spirit to create a communion of men with God and with one another. To bring this *koinonia* to perfection is God's eternal purpose. The Church exists to serve the fulfilment of this purpose when God will be all in all.[7]

This paragraph helps us understand what we saw in the arias of Bach and the baptism of Victorinus. Authority is actualized in the church when Christ is confessed; the Christ who is confessed is the one who has all authority. He bestows the Holy Spirit to bring human beings into communion with God and each other. Which is to say the work of the Holy Spirit is to bring about the leap across time that is present in authority, for the "leap" is made possible by the divine communion granted by the Holy Spirit in the midst of the church, which is, one could say, a sign of the communion of humanity not yet realized. The authority of Christ is enacted in the gathered assembly when Christ is confessed, preeminently in the personal confession of the individual who, confessing Christ, speaks authoritatively; she thus is, we could say, "authorized."

From this vantage-point one understands the structure of ARCIC's 1976 statement on authority in the church. From the concise

7 Anglican-Roman Catholic International Commission, *Authority in the Church I*, 1976, sec. 1; in *idem, The Final Report* (London: SPCK and Catholic Truth Society, 1982). Subsequent citations will be noted in the text as "*Authority I*."

one-paragraph introduction quoted above, the document turns first to speak of "Christian Authority," that is, the authority of Christian persons individually and collectively to speak and act in such a way that people "perceive the authoritative word of Christ" (*Authority I*, para. 3). Following Christian authority, the statement speaks of "Authority in the Church" which includes the authority of individuals bestowed with special gifts, among which is the ministry of *episcope* or oversight. Then the statement takes up how local churches are related to each other; here we find authority in the communion of churches. Finally, in the context of this nested and overlapping conciliar structure, questions of matters of faith can be addressed.

It would be an error to see this document as moving in a hierarchical upward direction, from (at the base) the authority of the individual Christian, upward to that of the local church or bishop, and further on to that of international authorities including whatever authority we might agree to recognize in the pope. The error would not only be to ignore that the lower must always recognize itself in the higher—although that is true, as we see in the necessity that authoritative acts be "received" (see *Authority I*, para. 6 on reception, and para. 18 for a delicate articulation of the church's indefectibility). Most fundamentally, a hierarchical reading would ignore that, in fact, this document works from the top downwards: from Christ who has been given all authority, to Christian persons who have authority because they confess Christ faithfully, and then downward to various institutional structures and decisions that exist to support and preserve that faith.

For what does it take to make possible the authoritative confession of faith in Christ? Arias do not exist on their own; even the most beautiful of them, sung as a solo performance in a program far removed from the *Passion* or the church, if such an aria is effective, evokes the context from which it came: the broader story of salvation, the corpus of Bach's work, the tradition of sacred music, and so forth. Arias, that is, are inextricably contextualized: they need the chorus, the conductor, the tradition, and the sacred story in order be what they are—in order to be authoritative. So we cannot have an individual confession of Christ that does not arise out of a eucharistic community. And we cannot have eucharistic community without the oversight of a bishop. And we cannot have a bishop who is not in communion with other bishops, nor a eucharistic community that is not in communion with other eucharistic communities. And we cannot have communities and bishops without some means of making authoritative determinations about the boundaries of Christian confession.[8] But all these things—authoritative doctrinal determinations, authoritative conciliar structures, authoritative persons with oversight of particular communities—all exist to make possible the one truly authoritative act, which is the confession of Christ, which like all authority is ineluctably personal.

ARCIC's 1976 statement on authority was followed by an *Elucidation* that it issued in 1981 along with a second statement, all of which were published in its *Final Report* of that year. Subsequently, a successor ARCIC commission revisited the subject with its 1999 statement, *Authority in the Church III: The Gift of Authority*.[9] Throughout these statements, observes the British ecumenist Mary Tanner, it is argued that authority is not optional; the church needs authority. But whose authority is it? Tanner writes: "ARCIC is clear that the primary authority for all Christians is Jesus Christ himself.... [T]he authority agenda is essentially about God's authority, given to the Son and, through the Son, to the Church, and made active in the Church through the power of the Holy Spirit. It is not the authority of bishops or councils, or of the Bishop of Rome."[10]

If we take this point seriously, we find two things. First, and not surprisingly, we find theological warrant for our long-standing claim that to have authority is to be under authority. The individual has authority because she is under the authority of Christ. Second, and perhaps surprisingly, we find a reversal of the identification of the one who is the authorized person. When considering social authority, we identified the conductor as the authority who makes possible the performance of the orchestra playing together. After all, it is she, the conductor, who takes the first bow at the end. By analogy, we might expect the bishop, or an international council of leading bishops, or a pope—in whatever form, some hierarchical structure—to be the authority who makes possible the "performances" of the church, whatever we think those to be. And by analogy with epistemic authority, we might expect those same hierarchical figures to be the ones who, authoritatively, point to the

8 I say "cannot," and yet we obviously do have all these things—individuals estranged from communities, communities estranged from their bishops, bishops estranged from one another, and Christian teaching in manifest confusion. Which is but to say, we have authority in disrepair. Yet even in its manifest imperfections, the church can reveal to us the true shape of authority.

9 The text may be found in many places, including the website of the Centro Pro Unione: http://www.prounione.urbe.it/dia-int/arcic/doc/e_arcicII_05.html.

10 Mary Tanner, "The ARCIC Dialogue and the Perception of Authority," *Journal of Anglican Studies* 1.2 (2003): 47–61; here, 51.

Truth. But the reality of authority in the church turns out to be rather differently ordered. It is the individual who is to have authority, and she has that authority, yes, thanks to the work of bishops and councils. But her relationship to them is not the relationship she has to Christ. She is most properly under *Christ's* authority—as, of course, bishops and councils also are.

Authority in the church, in other words, highlights for us an essential dynamic in the working out of authority. *The community is prior to the individual.* No person could have faith or come to any knowledge of truth without submitting to the authority of others. *And yet the community exists only in the individual to which it gives rise.* The individual, as it were, contains the community, even as she enacts, authoritatively, the faithful response of the community, which must be in an individual, to the faithfulness of the one who is the source of all the church's authority, namely the Son to whom all authority has been given.

Herbert McCabe prepares us for this conclusion in his discussion of the relationship of the individual person and the human species as a whole. He writes: "[S]ociety is not the product of individual people. On the contrary, individual people are the product of society." The error of contractarian thinking in political philosophy—that already-existing individuals enter into contracts together to make societies—lies in the fact that before you could be an individual you must "be already in possession of what only society could provide—institutions such as language, contract, agreement, and so on." Humans are rational beings, which means preeminently that we can talk with each other and articulate alternatives to the way things are. "Rationality," McCabe says, "is a special way of being in a group."[11]

And what is the special way of being in a group that comes about from our rationality? It is a complete transformation of "the notions of whole and part." When one is thinking of a mechanical construction, the parts get put together to make the whole. Doors and engines and tires and many other things, for instance, go together to make an automobile. We have the parts, and then we have the whole. But for rational beings, the whole has to be there first. For rational beings, the whole preexists the part. For example, you can't have language unless some society has given it to you. The "revolution," as McCabe calls it, that distinguishes the human grouping is marked by "language and rationality, the symbols in which she [the individual] can represent herself to herself."[12]

11 Herbert McCabe, *The Good Life* (London: Continuum, 2005), 26.

12 Ibid., 27.

So we should not be surprised to learn in the church, through such events as the sacrament of new birth or the faith-profession of the solo aria, that we *come to be* through community. We have seen, for instance in Chapter 2 above, that authority is necessary for society to exist, and thus authority is necessary for us human beings to flourish. The deeper truth is that such authority as society has, comes to its fulfillment when the individual becomes authoritative.

In like manner, the discussion of political authority in the previous chapter also brought us close to this conclusion. In O'Donovan's unfolding of the outlines of political authority he turns at the end to the problem of a collapsing regime, the demise of political authority. At such a juncture all is not lost, for the tradition of the community, the perpetuation of which is part of what political authority consists in, can be carried on by individuals who have been formed within that functioning political society. To repeat O'Donovan's theorem: "*the conscience of the individual members of a community is a repository of the moral understanding which shaped it, and may serve to perpetuate it in a crisis of collapsing morale or institution.*"[13] What happens here is that, in the absence of effective political authority, the authority of the individual is revealed. That authority is not political, but has something of political authority about it—and indeed has always had that authority, but it was not noticed when political authority was functioning well, when, that is, the morale and institutions of the community were effective. But in their decline, as in the periodic declines recorded in the Old Testament history of Israel, the authorized individual is uncovered; the prophet rises to speak truth and to bear witness of the tradition that made such individuals possible.

The Inescapable Difficulty of the Reading of Scripture: The Wisdom of Richard Hooker

When the Anglican-Roman Catholic International Commission in 1976 described authority as flowing from Christ to the individual and only then turned to the authority of bishops, councils, popes, and doctrinal statements, many of the responses raised the question "whether sufficient attention" had been given "to the primary authority of

13 *The Desire of the Nations*, 80; emphasis original.

Scripture."[14] In its *Elucidation* of 1981, and in its third statement on authority, the 1999 *Gift of Authority*, the Commission labored to increase its clarity about Scripture's authority. In the 1981 *Elucidation*, as Tanner summarizes it, Scripture has priority but is not "the sole and exclusive source of guidance" to the church. Going further, the 1999 *Gift of Authority* says that "within Tradition the Scriptures occupy a unique and normative place and belong to what has been given once for all"; that all the church's "teaching, preaching and action" is to be measured by them; that the Scriptures are "uniquely authoritative."[15]

Nonetheless, there remains always the question of how to read Scripture. ARCIC in its 1981 *Elucidation* framed the question as one of how "Tradition" (here capitalized) interacts with Scripture. One approach sees Tradition as the discovery, over time and in a variety of situations, of "riches and truths" that have always been contained in Scripture but which were previously undiscovered. Another approach, not necessarily contradictory to the first, sees the Holy Spirit as guiding "the Church into the fullness of truth" by "draw[ing] upon everything in human experience and thought" in order to give a full and wide application to "the content of the revelation" of Scripture. Whether either approach concludes with truth is a judgment that must be deferred to "reception by the whole Church," because "*neither approach is immune from the possibility of error.*"[16]

ARCIC thus raises what I am calling the inescapable difficulty of the reading of Scripture. It does so under the rubric of the problem of the relationship of Scripture and Tradition. But it is a problem native to the very nature of Scripture itself. To see this problem developed in masterful detail, I turn to Richard Hooker (1553/4–1600), whose book, *Of the Laws of Ecclesiastical Polity*,[17] proved to be a classic defense of the Elizabethan settlement of the government, liturgy, and structure of the Church of England against Puritan and Roman Catholic

14 Anglican-Roman Catholic International Commission, *Authority in the Church: Elucidation*, 1981, sec. 1; in *The Final Report*.

15 Tanner, "The ARCIC Dialogue," 52; the latter quotes are from *The Gift of Authority*, sec. 19.

16 ARCIC, *Elucidation*, 1981, sec. 2; emphasis added.

17 Hereinafter referred to as *Laws*. The text has recently been established in Richard Hooker, *Of the Laws of Ecclesiastical Polity*, ed. Georges Edelen et al., vols. 1–4 of the Folger Library Edition of the Works of Richard Hooker (Cambridge, Mass.: Harvard University Press, 1977–82). Notwithstanding this important scholarly achievement, I will quote instead, for the sake of convenience of reading, from the text as edited by John Keble, 3rd ed. (Oxford: Oxford University Press, 1845).

alternatives. Hooker's conservative wisdom articulates an Anglican "gold standard" of sorts which subsequent generations have continually mined for insight.[18] Such is my intention here.

The question of the authority of Scripture arises within the church, and the church is a society. It turns out to have and need social authority just as do other societies. The lines of the argument will not be strange. As with Yves Simon, so Hooker would grant that authority has a substitutionary function. Human beings "generally" need to be constrained to do what they should do; therefore, to apply this to the church, prelates are necessary (*Laws* VII.xviii.5). Yet this constraining power is occasioned by sin and would be unnecessary "if we were all such as we should be," and thus constraining from sin can hardly be the whole of authority's function. There is, for instance, the necessity that authority make decisions on "matters indifferent," which decisions are needed for the church to carry on. Much of Hooker's discussion in the *Laws* pertains to the appropriateness of the church authoritatively establishing customs and rites—and in general what he calls "order"—the particulars of which are not prescribed by Scripture. In terms of social authority, we may see such determinations as authority deciding on the means to achieve, and willing the matter of, the common good—here, the ability of the church to attain its end of proclamation, salvation, praise, and so forth.

Hooker discerns that those who would dismiss the power of the church to decide on matters of order are putting their own reason in the place of the authority of the church; and thus they undermine that authority, with the result being the diminishment of the ability of the church to be a society. He does concede—indeed he emphasizes—that if the church is doctrinally in error (a position which for Hooker means the teaching of doctrines that are contrary to that which Scripture lays out clearly or to that which can be clearly deduced from Scripture), then the individual must speak prophetically in opposition to authority. But in matters of ceremony, as in all matters on which Scripture does not speak clearly—he instances such things as the use of church-bells and the baptism of infants[19]—the church has the necessary function of making authoritative determinations that are appropriate for

18 On Hooker as a "conservative" in political philosophy (which, need I say, is hardly to be identified with a conservative in contemporary politics?), see Anthony Quinton, *The Politics of Imperfection: The Religious and Secular Traditions of Conservative Thought in England from Hooker to Oakeshott* (London: Faber and Faber, 1978).

19 See *Laws* II.vii.2.

the time, and which might also be changed. We see the operative distinction in the following passage.

> The Church hath authority to establish that for an order at one time, which at another time it may abolish, and in both may do well. But that which in doctrine the Church doth now deliver rightly as a truth, no man will say that it may hereafter recall, and as rightly avouch the contrary. Laws touching matter of order are changeable, by the power of the Church; articles concerning doctrine not so.... [In matters both of doctrine and order] what Scripture doth plainly deliver, to that the first place of credit and obedience is due; the next whereunto is whatsoever any man can necessarily conclude by force of reason; after these the voice of the Church succeedeth. That which the Church by her ecclesiastical authority shall probably think and define to be true or good, must in congruity of reason overrule all other inferior judgments whatsoever. (*Laws* V.viii.2)

The rub comes with Hooker's distinction of order and doctrine. We might well ask how it is to be determined whether a point of dispute belongs to order or to doctrine—as, in Chapter 3, we encountered the difficulty of drawing a line between core doctrine and matters indifferent.[20] In practice, the church's authority will have to decide that higher-level question as well (although by Hookerian principles dissent from decisions judged to involve doctrinal error would continue to be required). There is no escaping the church's authority (as Hooker states in a discussion of the use of the cross in baptism) over

> traditions, ordinances made in the prime of Christian religion, established with that authority which Christ hath left to his Church for matters indifferent, and in that consideration requisite to be observed, till like authority see just and reasonable cause to alter them. (*Laws* V.lxv.2)

Still the epistemic question remains. How can it be determined, authoritatively, that a doctrine is clearly stated in Scripture or immediately deducible therefrom? How, that is, can we know that the church authority is truly handing on that which is contained in Scripture?

20 Some arguments for women's ordination urge the consideration that who can be ordained is a matter of order and thus within the freedom of the church's authority to change. And some arguments in defense of the tradition of an all-male priesthood have argued that the question is one of doctrine, and thus not within the freedom of the church to change. Both of these views maintain the Hookerian distinction of order and doctrine and the Hookerian view that the church has the right and necessity to decide matters of order and to change them whenever it appears, as he would say, "convenient."

Hooker faces this question. While he emphatically ascribes Scripture a preeminent place in all knowledge of truth concerning doctrine, he points out that, not only does Scripture not say everything, it may not be a simple matter to determine what Scripture does in fact say. Thus authority is necessary, both to acquire the skills needed to read Scripture correctly, and also to perpetuate the knowledge of the truth that is held by tradition.

We see this, for example, in *Laws* II.vii.5, where while attacking the view that in matters of divinity human authority is of no weight whatsoever and the authority of Scripture is everything, Hooker affirms that Scripture is the most certain, the least fallible, of all authorities. Nonetheless, he acknowledges other authorities that we might call external or impersonal. Outside of Scripture, Hooker says, the most certain things are those that present themselves immediately to us: things, in short, that we see. Then, of only slightly less certainty, we have those things that are necessary conclusions, what we might call the productions of reason operating upon premises given as certain. And beneath all this, Hooker places conclusions that we accept as probable. Thus in descending order we have these authorities: Scripture, facts, necessary deductions, and probable deductions.

This is a hierarchy of external epistemological authorities, with Scripture at the summit. And these authorities are commended to us because we have intellectual passions: "the mind of man desireth evermore to know the truth according to the most infallible certainty which the nature of things can yield" (*Laws* II.vii.5). Truth is the lure that draws forth our desire to know. Yet, having affirmed that Scripture is the most certain of all authorities, Hooker turns the matter inside out by raising the difficulty of *knowing that Scripture is an authority at all*, much less the authority that yields "the most infallible certainty." We need a human authority to attest to the authority of Scripture: and this is the epistemic authority exercised within the church, which authority exists despite the sin of those who exercise it.

> [U]tterly to infringe the force and strength of man's testimony were to shake the very fortress of God's truth. For whatsoever we believe concerning salvation by Christ, although the Scripture be therein the ground of our belief; yet the authority of man is, if we mark it, the key which openeth the door of entrance into the knowledge of the Scripture. The Scripture could not teach us the things that are of God, unless we did credit men who have taught us that the words of Scripture do signify those things. Some way therefore, notwithstanding man's infirmity, yet his authority may enforce assent. (*Laws* II.vii.3)

Hooker calls upon his opponents to recognize what he takes to be an obvious fact, that "God hath endued [some people] with principal gifts to aspire unto knowledge by; whose exercises, labours, and divine studies he hath so blessed that the world for their great and rare skill that way hath them in singular admiration." He asks by what daring of intellect would we reject their judgment? "For mine own part," Hooker says, "I dare not so lightly esteem of the Church, and of the principal pillars therein" (*Laws* II.vii.4).

The church then must have epistemic authority that is human authority, persons who carry out the necessary function within the society that is the church to acquire knowledge of the truth as pertains to divinity. From this a further question arises: how might that knowledge be conveyed? Hooker confirms (as Polanyi would agree) that knowledge is conveyed by the acquisition of skills through study with those who are acknowledged to be proficient. Against his Puritan opponents, Hooker denies that "matters divine" differ in this regard from other subjects (*Laws* II.vii.4). It is not a straightforward matter to know what it is that Scripture says. True, some things are set forth clearly by Scripture. Yet by far a greater number of things are not set forth so, but must be drawn out from Scripture with some care. Here, as in most areas of life, we are aware of there being people whose manner of life causes us to trust them and their affirmations; if they say that Scripture affirms such a thing, then we have reason to trust their conclusion. We say, they "open" the Scripture to us (as Jesus opened the Scriptures on the road to Emmaus, see Lk. 24.13ff.); they have authority. Hooker affirms "the credit of learned men's judgments in opening that truth, which by being conversant in the Apostles' writings they have themselves from thence learned" (*Laws* II.vii.6)—provided, always, that their teachings do not plainly contradict Scripture or entail irrationalities in their reasoning.

Running through Hooker is a judicious trust given to the authority of the church, which is a trust in traditions that is in addition to whatever other warrants said traditions might have in their favor. He writes, concerning an ecclesiastical law, that even if divine law gave no positive requirement for that law, nor was it called for by "any invincible argument" of reason, nor was the law necessary for reason of public convenience, nonetheless, "the very authority of the Church itself, at the least in such cases, may give so much credit to her own laws, as to make their sentence touching fitness and conveniency weightier than any bare and naked conceit to the contrary" (*Laws* V.viii.5). He has granted that the church has authority to change traditions (but not doctrine); however, the bare fact of the church having a tradition is a factor in favor of its continuance. This trust given to the authority of tradition is grounded in Hooker's "conservative" appreciation of the limits of human rationality. Anthony Quinton has said that the "conservative's principle" in political philosophy is arguably "not itself political but rather epistemological."[21] Quinton finds in Hooker a "heav[y] load" carried by the "intellectual imperfection of man," in that "the limits of human reason imply that [the] form [of government] should be determined in a concrete, practical way, on considerations of circumstantial expediency and in reliance on tradition." The Puritan opponents of Hooker were guilty of "a cognitive sin," namely, "intellectual pride."[22] The Puritans thought the traditions of the church were of no weight; they would apply their own reason directly to the Scriptures and reach all conclusions in isolation from any need for epistemic authority.[23]

The epistemological reserve, the humility that underlies Hooker's argument—it is not limited to the acquisition of skills. As in Polanyi, so for Hooker, the need for trust in authority—in, to be clear, *persons* who bear authority—is never transcended. In an extended section discussing the place of human authority in reason, Hooker shows that such authority has positive weight, not only "with the simpler sort" of person, but also with "the learneder and wiser."

> The reason why the simpler sort are moved with authority is the conscience of their own ignorance; whereby it cometh to pass that having learned men in admiration, they rather fear to dislike them than know wherefore they should allow and follow their judgments. Contrariwise with them that are skilful authority is much more strong and forcible; because they only are able to discern how just cause there is why to some men's authority so much should be attributed.... And therefore not orators only with the people, but even the very profoundest disputers in all faculties have hereby often with the best learned prevailed most. (*Laws* II.vii.2)

Hooker would agree with Polanyi that the more one advances in knowledge, the more one recognizes the need for authority.

21 Quinton, *The Politics of Imperfection*, 13.

22 Ibid., 28.

23 Quinton may be wrong to suggest, with such language as "intellectual imperfection," that a perfectly good human being would not need to acknowledge epistemic authority. But why call our need to trust others in order to arrive at truth an "imperfection"? One might as well call it our nature, or our species' distinctive greatness.

Thus Hooker shows the essential functions of authority in the church and in theology. Authority is needed for the achievement of the common good of the church as a society. And authority is needed for the members of the church to come to knowledge of divine truth. In both cases, the authority is human authority. Analogously to Polanyi, Hooker has allowed the possibility of error on the part of authority, when it speaks on doctrinal matters. Yet his epistemic humility would make an individual Christian cautious about acting upon her judgment that church authorities had committed doctrinal error—cautious, but not by any means incapacitated.

The argument of this chapter to this point has entailed the claim that the church helps us see clearly that the point of authority—social, epistemic, and political—is the raising up of an individual who speaks truth authoritatively. That is, we need authority to flourish as human beings, but that very flourishing entails our being authorized. Then, because the Scriptures are distinctive to the church, it has been necessary to look to their authority. In doing so, we seem to have covered again old ground. For instance, like any society, the church must have persons who have social and epistemological authority. And however much we assert the authority of the Scriptures, there remains the inescapable difficulty that they must be read. But we must not stop here with the authorized individual in the midst of the community who speaks truthfully. For it is not only that we cannot escape the difficulty that Scriptures must be read, but, being read, they must give shape to the one who hears them. How does this formation occur? And what is the character of the life of the individual who rises to sing the aria—can we see how her life is a flourishing human life?

To approach answers to these questions, I will return once again to the claim that the point of all these authorities—the point of the church's social authority, and the end of the church's epistemic authority—is the authorization of the believing individual.

The Reading of Scripture and the Making of the Authorized Individual

If we follow Hooker while employing the terminology of this book, we will say something like the following. For church teaching to be authoritative it must be grounded in Scripture; yet, since Scripture is not self-interpreting, it is necessary that there be epistemic authority not only for one to learn the bare fact that Scripture is to be trusted and to acquire the pedagogical basics of reading it; there must also be epistemic authority all the way to the end, as those who are specially able to "open" the Scriptures continue to do so. In this light I now consider a peculiarity of the structure of what was traditional worship amongst Anglicans. I follow this path not as an exercise in nostalgia, although it is the case that the traditional worship I intend to describe is seldom found anymore. Nor is this special pleading upon the part of an author who happens to be an Episcopalian. For within the worship peculiarity that I am about to describe there is embodied a belief about the relation of authority and Scripture, and a implicit view about the authorization of the Christian believer, which will continue to have relevance whatever may happen to the troubled churches of the Anglican Communion.

Traditional Anglican public worship has taken the form of Morning Prayer and Evening Prayer. In both of these services, commonly called "the daily office," the basic structure includes preparatory material including a confession of sin, then the reading of Psalms, two Lessons from Scripture, the Apostles' Creed, and prayers.[24] At the center of the daily office are the Lessons, one from the Old Testament, one from the New. The rubric concerning the Lessons is the longest and most exacting of any rubric in the office. I quote it from the 1559 Book:

> *Then shall be read two Lessons distinctly with a loud voice that the people may hear. The first of the Old Testament, the second of the New, like as they be appointed in the Calendar, except there be proper Lessons assigned for that day. The minister that readeth the Lesson standing and turning him so as he may best be heard of all such as be present. And before every Lesson, the minister shall say thus.* The first, second, third, *or* fourth chapter of Genesis, *or* Exodus, Matthew, Mark, *or other like, as is appointed in the Calendar. And in the end of every chapter he shall say,* Here endeth *such a* chapter of *such a book.*[25]

The Calendar to which this rubric refers was an orderly arrangement of the books of the Bible to be read, chapter by chapter, through the year. In the 1559 Book, for example, January saw the entire book of Genesis

24 What I give as the standard form has been established in most versions of the Book of Common Prayer since the Elizabethan volume of 1559. There are variations; the daily office in the first Book of Common Prayer (1548/49), for instance, lacked the confession of sin and the Apostles' Creed. A valuable resource for the U.S. Episcopal tradition is Paul V. Marshall, *Prayer Book Parallels: The Public Services of the Church Arranged for Comparative Study*, Anglican Liturgy in America, vol. 1 (New York: Church Hymnal Corporation, 1989).

25 John E. Booty, ed., *The Book of Common Prayer 1559: The Elizabethan Prayer Book* (Charlottesville, Va.: The University Press of Virginia, for the Folger Shakespeare Library, 1976), 53; the red type of the original has been italicized above.

read, one chapter at Morning Prayer, another at Evening Prayer (skipping only Chapter 10), plus the first nine chapters of Exodus. In addition, at Morning Prayer the 28 chapters of Matthew were read, while Evening Prayer undertook the 16 chapters of Romans followed by the first 12 chapters of 1 Corinthians. These sequential readings, chapter by chapter, of the books of the Bible, were interrupted only by the occasional major feast, for example, the Epiphany, and, in the case of the first Lesson (but rarely the second), by Sundays.[26]

These provisions show how the authority of the church is at work in traditional Anglican worship. The church as a society exercises its authority by prescribing a structure for worship—the daily offices of Morning and Evening Prayer, each having at its center two readings of Scripture, covering both the Old and New Testaments and, over the course of a year, covering most of the canon of the Bible. The church's authority is also shown in the persons who carry out these instructions, organizing the worship for a local parish and officiating, singing, and reading the assigned texts. The authority of Scripture, taken as foundational, is seen in the deference given to it by the church's structures, placing it at the center of the liturgy.

The Anglican prayer book tradition has looked to antiquity as its ground for this practice. The Preface to the 1548/49 Book of Common Prayer provides a classic statement. Here it is asserted that "the auncient fathers…so ordered the matter, that the whole Bible (or the greatest parte thereof) should be read ouer once in the yeare, intendyng thereby, that the Cleargie…should…be stirred up to godlines themselfes…[and] that the people (by daily hearyng of holy scripture read in the Churche) should continuallye profite more and more in the knowledge of God, and bee the more inflamed with the loue of his true religion."[27]

26 See Booty, *The Book of Common Prayer* 1559, 27–47.

27 Ephraim Radner has referred to the "ethos of formative scripturalism" that Thomas Cranmer implanted in the 1548/49 Book of Common Prayer. Cranmer drew upon and favorably referred to "antyquitye" and the "auncient" or "olde fathers" of the church (as in the Preface quoted above), not because, Radner says, he wished to draw upon tradition for its own sake, nor because of the doctrine he found there expressed. Rather, Cranmer found in the early church "a faithful model of scriptural exposition within the 'divine service' of clergy and people." Radner calls this "'pragmatic exemplarism,' the historically proven virtue of scriptural conformance." Radner thus states Cranmer's view: "If the past deserved to be followed, it was only because the past had read the Scriptures, presented them in whole to the people, and practiced their formative powers in an ordered and effective manner." Ephraim Radner, "The Scriptural Community: Authority in Anglicanism," in Radner and Turner, *The Fate of Communion*, 90–112; here, 100–1.

For those unfamiliar with Anglican worship, the daily office may seem odd for a point that is missing from it. There is no mention of a sermon. Morning and evening, day in and day out, the Scriptures are read at length. They are to be read clearly, so that the people present may hear them distinctly. But there is no provision for commentary upon them. *The daily office is structured so that Scripture may be read, and heard, without mediating interpretation.* There are behind-the-scenes interpretations, as it were: the decision to read *this* rather than *that,* and most fundamental of all the decision to acknowledge Scripture's central authoritative place. But to the "reading" of Scripture, that is to the authoritative response to the proclamation of the saving deeds, that is not a function absorbed by the authoritative structures of the church. The authoritative response of the authorized individual who will be able to proclaim her faith in Christ—this is being formed by the practice of the serial and daily reading of Scripture in and for the congregation of the faithful.

I am not saying that the individual is left without interpretive guidance, for individuals always arise out of communities. Besides the daily office, the Book of Common Prayer has provided for a service of Holy Communion, traditionally offered at least on Sundays, within which there is to be a "sermon, homily, or exhortation."[28] Sermons have also been known to follow the daily office at certain times; thus the occasional service title, "Morning Prayer with Sermon." There are other guides: the catechism of the Prayer Book, the rich tradition of composed prayers, the creeds used in liturgy (the Nicene at Communion, Apostles' at every daily office, and sometimes the Athanasian[29]), the Articles of Religion; not to mention the conformation of character and belief that comes from living and working with fellow Christians. Yet all this, in the end, has the ultimate purpose of making the individual *authorized.*

How this authorization occurs is as varied as there are people and situations in life. But we can easily sketch some of the possibilities. Through the obedient listening to the Scriptures, a father may come to repentance and conversion of life as regards his treatment of his family. For instance, he hears the parable of the prodigal son and finds himself convicted of not having a merciful heart, and in repentance he

28 See, for instance, page 251 of Booty, ed., *The Book of Common Prayer 1559.*

29 The 1559 Book called for the Athanasian Creed to be said on 13 specified days, at Morning Prayer, in place of the Apostles' Creed. See Booty, ed., *The Book of Common Prayer 1559,* 64.

turns to the Lord, calls upon the Holy Spirit, and endeavors to amend his life. Conviction, sorrow, repentance, turning, amendment: this pattern of life for sinful folk is one of the themes that cannot but be heard when one attends to the Scriptures in the community of the church.

Another pattern is joy. A woman is bearing a child within her. Her pregnancy, like all pregnancies, has been an opportunity for anxiety. Will my family have enough of the material goods of life to care for this child? Will I have enough wisdom and patience to lead this child in the right way, or will my parenting fall short and perhaps even be harmful? Will this pregnancy turn out to injure my own health? These and a hundred such questions are universal. But through the formative scripturalism of the church, this woman also knows well several characters who lived thousands of years ago, knows them as if they were her neighbors. She knows Sarah, to whom the Lord gave a child when she was 90. She knows Hannah, who wept over her infertility. She knows Rachel, who wept over children who died too young. She knows Elizabeth and Mary. She thinks too of what she prays every day: "Give us this day our daily bread." And so she puts aside her anxiety and does not invest her thoughts in how she will act in the future, but rather sings a song of praise. Her child (like every child) is from the Lord, and she will trust the Lord and give thanks to the Lord, this day and every day. In her life, anxiety is replaced by joy.

One never knows what connections will be made between the Scriptures and the life of the faithful, for the reason that flourishing human life is vast with possibilities beyond our reckoning, and the Holy Spirit blows where he will. One woman, shaped by decades of attending to the Scriptures in community, will rise up and cross an ocean to place herself and her skills at the service of the poor. Another man will travel nowhere, but turn in care to a neighbor whom he had previously walked past. There will be hearts broken in remorse and rebuilt as stronger friends. Misunderstandings will be exposed, and some will work to set things right. There is no end to it, because there is no being finished with the command to love your neighbor as yourself.

When we see Scripture read in public, in sequence, with twice-daily frequency, without accompanying interpretation, we can see a plain fact: that the truly authorized person (and since authority is personal, the true authority) can only be the one who is listening. She is now but a member of the chorus who, following the recitation of Scripture, will stand to join in the *Benedictus* or *Magnificat* or other prescribed canticle. But the hope of the universe is that she is being prepared to sing her aria. And when she does, we will rejoice in her authority.

Judge for Yourselves: The Church as the Locus of Authoritative Non-judgment

What, again, does this authorized individual look like? What does it mean to have authority? It means, we might say, that the Scriptures have been internalized. The individual with authority is able to rise from the community, which remains present within her, and speak and do what needs to be done in the particulars of the situation at hand. So an authorized individual may be doing any of the many things we expect to see amongst Christian people. She may be praising God, giving a personal account of what God has done for her; she may be performing evangelism, which is the proclamation in word or deed of what God has done in creating and redeeming the world and offering promise for the ultimate meaningfulness of human life. We may see her as a corporate executive, creating opportunities for the increase of wealth and goods in society. Or we may see her in some of the many other mini-societies that people are involved in: medical, educational, cultural, and so forth, not forgetting the important societies of family and neighborhood. *We will not expect to see her as an "authority" within any of these societies (although she may be one), and in particular we will not expect to see her as an "authority" in the church.* For what we have learned from the church is that the structures of authority, which are necessary, and the persons who exercise authority, who are also necessary, ultimately serve the authorization of the individual believer who bears the society within her. Which is why we turn naturally to the metaphor of "internalization." But there can be other metaphors.

We might, for instance, think of the spatial orientation of the believer to the Scriptures. Exploring questions that arise in practical life, O'Donovan suggests we think of the Scriptures as standing behind the believer. For other questions, of course, the Scriptures are in front—the textual question, for instance, of what the Scriptures objectively say. And for such questions we turn to persons with epistemic authority; experts, for instance, on manuscripts and the like. But for the questions of practical action, of what I should do in this situation at hand, the scriptural text "sheds light forward upon us." It gives us "categories and analogies" by which we can probe ourselves and our situation. For instance: "The Scripture tells us not to bear false witness against our neighbor. Whether *this* particular ambiguous statement we have it in mind to make will be false, or merely discreet, is something that the Scripture will not tell us; we must *judge that for ourselves* with the aid of the Holy Spirit."[30]

Whether we think of them as internalized by the believer or somehow standing behind her, projecting light forward, the Scriptures have importantly contributed to the authorization of the individual. We can gain some purchase on the difference this makes to authority if we consider the question of judgment. The necessary authorities in social, epistemological, and political arenas are involved in the exercise of judgment. They must make decisions for the good of the society. A conductor makes several judgments that are necessary for, and aim to the production of, the music of the orchestra; without those judgments, there would be no music to be heard. Similarly epistemological authorities are necessary for the apprehension of truth and for any continuing growth in understanding. And political authorities, perhaps most obviously of all, exist to provide the discrimination between what is right and what is wrong, between guilt and innocence, between what tends to establish justice for the community's future and what works against it. Within the church, there are those who have a similar, and equally necessary, function of judgment. Admittedly, in various churches the persons who perform this function are variously chosen: sometimes pope and curia, sometimes synods; sometimes bishops only, sometimes elected laity and clergy together; sometimes centralized, sometimes dispersed. Yet in whatever mode, these persons make judgments that are necessary for the church as a society to continue. They decide on rites of worship, on membership, on church plantings, on statements of doctrine, and on the many other things that are seen as needed for the advancement of the mission of the church. They decide, it seems: which is to say, they make judgments: which is to say, they have authority in that sense.

But the secret exposed by the church, that authority flows from the Father to the Son, and from the Son by means of the Spirit to the believer—the secret, that is to say, that the person with true authority is the one who *listens* to the Scriptures and then "*reads*" them in her life of praise and service—this secret manifests itself in the kind of judgment that the authorized individual makes. *She judges for herself.*

Jesus famously commanded his disciples, "Judge not, that ye be not judged" (Mt. 7.1). Just so, many Christians ordinarily reckon it as a

30 Oliver O'Donovan, *Church in Crisis: The Gay Controversy and the Anglican Communion* (Eugene, Ore.: Cascade Books, 2008), 59, emphasis added.

Christian moral failing to pass judgment, even in the face of matters where judgment would seem to be rather clear-cut. There are passages of Scripture in which Jesus seems to command the abandonment of judgment—and thus the setting aside of authority. This is a complex matter. Is Jesus' involvement in the story of the woman caught in adultery (Jn 8.3–11) a matter of the setting-aside of judgment, or the imposition of a higher form of judgment? Both views have seemed plausible to saintly theologians—and church authorities![31] Yet over against "judge not" we need to put Jesus' equally emphatic, judge "of yourselves" (Lk. 12.57; cf. 1 Cor. 10.15, 11.13). It is hypocritical, Jesus says, to claim to be his follower and at the same time turn to a secular magistrate for judgment. True judgment, which comes with true authority, is already in Jesus and in those who have responded to his call to follow him.

True judgment is in Jesus because it has been given him by his Father (see, for example, Jn 8.16, within the passage that, in the received text, follows upon the story of the woman taken in adultery). Here we cannot avoid speaking explicitly about the Trinity—a task that could be left implicit in the earlier chapters of this book. The second "person" of God "proceeds" timelessly and eternally from the Father. He is God's speech, or God's reason, or God's thought; he is God's image. We cannot know what it means for God, who is no being in the universe and who cannot be imagined by any created being, not only to be the source of things existing but also to have the thought/word/image of himself. But we do know one thing: for God to be God, and not a creature, he cannot have parts. And so, by the paradoxical logic of trinitarian thought (unimaginable and yet not self-contradictory), we must say that the thought/word/image God has of himself cannot be different from God himself. If God thinks about himself, that thought cannot be a creature or an emanation; the thought God has of himself simply is God. So the Son is God.

Similarly, if God takes enjoyment in himself, if God finds himself delightful, that joy or delight, again, must simply be God. So the Holy Spirit, often spoken of as the love of the Father and the Son, is God and no property or emanation or creature of God.

31 The paradigmatic contrast can be seen between Ambrose (339–97), who saw Jesus as effecting the suspension of judgment, and Augustine (354–430), who in contrast took Jesus to be about the business of a higher and correcting court. For references and discussion, see O'Donovan, *The Desire of the Nations*, 200, 202; see also ibid., 256–9.

We need, finally, to recall the main point of the doctrine of the Incarnation: that the man Jesus of Nazareth is identical with the second person of the Trinity. He is God's Word. This means that he has two natures, which means we can talk about him in two different ways. We can say things about Jesus that are true of God, and we can say things about him that are true of human beings. "That Jesus over there holds all things in being," for instance, is true; as is "That Jesus over there slept well last night."[32]

Everything that is the Father's has been given to Jesus; and so the Father, who has authority over all things, has given his authority to his Son. Thus Jesus can say, "All authority in heaven and earth has been given to me" (Mt. 28.18). Nonetheless he is also under authority, as the centurion perceptively acknowledged (Lk. 7.8; cf. Mt. 8.9).[33] The deep meaning of Jesus being both *in* and *under* authority thus has a trinitarian foundation: he receives authority from his Father which means he has the authority of the Father.

For to be given authority is to share in authority. In St. Mark's Gospel, when Jesus sends out the twelve in pairs, Mark writes that he "gave them authority [*exousia*] over the unclean spirits" (Mk 6.7; NRSV). But in the event, the twelve went out (as commanded) and did "cast out many demons" (as authorized), yet their work did not stop there. They also preached repentance and healed the sick (Mk 6.12f.). Preaching repentance and curing disease were things Jesus did also, performances whereby Jesus showed his authorization from the Father. Thus those whom Jesus authorizes are seen to share in his authority, even to the extent of extemporizing how to do so: the healings done by the twelve were accompanied by the use of oil, a material Jesus had neither

32 These paragraphs are a painfully abbreviated sketch of basic trinitarian and incarnational theology. I would refer my readers who are interested in fuller accounts to Herbert McCabe's essays "Aquinas on the Trinity" and "Aquinas on the Incarnation," in *God Still Matters* (London: Continuum, 2002). The thought of Robert W. Jenson is both dense and rewarding here; see his *Systematic Theology*, vol. 1, *The Triune God* (Oxford: Oxford University Press, 1997). For a selection of fundamental theological texts from Aquinas's *Summa theologiae* with notes that are exceedingly helpful, see Frederick Christian Bauerschmidt, *Holy Teaching: Introducing the* Summa Theologiae *of St. Thomas Aquinas* (Grand Rapids, Mich.: Brazos Press, 2005).

33 The Authorized Version translates the Greek *kai* as "also"; other translations omit it. Yet even if we hear the centurion say only "I am a man under authority," the implied parallel stands, namely, that Jesus similarly can command because Jesus is similarly under authority.

used himself nor commanded to them.[34] To be under authority, to receive authority, to exercise authority—from none of these angles does authority have to do with willful command. From every angle, authority is a sharing. An aspect of communion, may we say?

For, in point of fact, in what manner do we speak of the authorized individual, within the congregation of the faithful, as having authority? We do so by means of the Holy Spirit. It is the Holy Spirit who incorporates the individual into Christ, both initially in baptism and continually as the grace of baptism is sustained. The individual who arises from the congregation of the faithful, having been conformed to a life itself formed by the unmediated yet communal reading of Scripture: she is under authority because by the Holy Spirit she has made the faithful response to God in Christ. And it is she about whom we want to say, as we round up our delving into the trinitarian mystery, that she judges for herself.

For to judge for yourself is to submit to the judgment of the Holy Spirit, and to make that judgment your own. It is an act of obedience. But obedience is not what it is commonly taken to be. The word derives from the Latin "audire," which is "to listen, to hear." True obedience has nothing to do with submission of a rebellious will, and everything to do with practical intelligence. First it is communities, as McCabe tells us, that are obedient—and only then can an individual be so. Obedience, indeed, belongs to "superiors" as much as to anyone: it is the practice of learning from each other, and in the church no one is exempt from the need to do that. Ultimately, "our obedience is the obedience of Christ. Christ lived his whole life and died in total *obedience* to his Father and yet was *equal* to his Father. This is the Mystery of the Trinity.... [O]ur obedience, our relationship to the community, is not just *like* the relationship of God the Son to God the Father; it *is* a sharing into that relationship."[35] To obey, we may say, is to listen to the judgment of the Holy Spirit that has already been given, and in that judgment to find freedom—to be authorized.

This is the heart of the mystery uncovered in the church's formative scripturalism. Those who listen to the Word hear and are guided

34 See Robert H. Gundry, *Mark: A Commentary on His Apology for the Cross* (Grand Rapids, Mich.: Eerdmans, 1993), 310: Jesus "heals with his word, his touch, and his spittle. The disciples' use of oil, a substance foreign to themselves, shows that it is only through his power that they heal."

35 Herbert McCabe, "Obedience," in *God Matters* (London: Geoffrey Chapman, 1987; repr. London: Continuum, 2005), 226–34; here, 233.

by the Holy Spirit to make the judgment of God their own judgment, and thereby to judge for themselves. "The society that refrains from judging," writes O'Donovan, "is a society that has felt the need for judgment, has cried to God for judgment, and has seen it revealed in Christ; and believing what it has seen, it has judged for itself." Such feeling, crying, seeing, believing, and judging are essential to the life of the church, and they show "the necessary character of social coexistence," O'Donovan tells us, but as "a divine summons to human freedom, not as a closed and coercive system."[36] From the outside, of course, authority in the church can been seen only sociologically, and thus only from the top down, yes, in a system that might well be "closed and coercive." But come sing this Passion, and you may rise to praise in freedom.

I put it in brief. In the church the authorized individual manifests judgment, which has ever been a signal means of authority manifesting itself. But this judgment is the paradox of non-judgment, which turns out to be the authorization to judge for oneself.

36 O'Donovan, *The Ways of Judgment*, 238, 241.

Chapter 6

AUTHORITY AND ERROR: DISPUTED AUTHORITY

The Bind We are in

That authority is necessary for human flourishing is no guarantee that authority will be exercised wisely. There are, in fact, many causes on account of which authority may go astray. First off, there is garden-variety mendacity, the failure of an authority to be true. This is what is condemned under the name of hypocrisy, as we see in the leader who claims to do everything he does out of a spirit of self-sacrifice for the sake of the common good—"All I want is to serve the American people," he might say—while in reality, in his heart, he has no concern for the common good at all. We speak of mendacious folk as abusing or betraying the trust that they have as authorities; for to be a true authority is indeed to exercise care that truth is grasped and the human good is actualized in the particulars of the situation at hand. A wicked authority is, in fact, nothing but a sham authority, a pretense, a simulacrum of the real thing. Ahab lusted to seize the vineyard of his neighbor Naboth. His wife asked the rhetorical question: Are you not the king of Israel? The power in the king's command was mustered to frame and execute Naboth and then the king took his vineyard. Thereby, ironically, it was proven that Ahab was no true king (see 1 Kgs 21).

Yet there remain many non-mendacious, non-hypocritical ways that authority can err. We have seen that all authority is personal, that authority is a performative concept, something that exists (like an aria) only in its actualization. But human persons are necessarily limited. Our lives are embedded in the realities of time and space, which means we perceive the world with perspective, from within; we can construct no Babylonian tower from which to survey the universe all at once as a whole. Embedded in time, we are constrained to act "in time" in two senses: our actions are, first, temporal, and second, they must be done "in time," before it is too late. All of which means we cannot forestall indefinitely every decision while we await yet more information, more data, prior to concretizing the possibilities before us into a definitive action. No, we must act ineluctably within limitations of perspective and temporality, the clock ticking to remind us that it is the human fate to make decisions without being able to see or understand everything.

Authorities, that is to say, can and do err because they lack comprehensiveness of vision. They lack it because they are human, and no human can see as God sees. One might then wonder if we could dispense with authority. Since authority cannot but err, must we have it?

It is, I judge, the common assumption in Western societies today that we can and should live with as little authority as possible. Jeffrey Stout's perceptive historical and philosophical analysis, *The Flight from Authority*, pegs the matter in its subtitle: *Religion, Morality, and the Quest for Autonomy*.[1] It has been our cultural project for some time to think of ourselves as living in a cultural period that is, in the temporal sense, "after authority." In our post-authority world, the ideal is to be autonomous, and that is to be free. Freedom then is assumed to mean *freedom from authority* particularly in such matters as philosophy, religion, and morality. The liberator from authority is often taken to be modern science. Bertrand Russell in 1952 wrote of science's "triumphs" as being "due to the substitution of observation and inference for authority." Liberation comes to us when we leave authority behind. On the other hand, Russell averred, "[e]very attempt to revive authority in intellectual matters is a retrograde step." Thus a key blessing that science bestows is the ability to live with the free and open inquiry of science, and that is, according to Russell, to live with science's probabilities, rather than having one's life based on "the delusive support of subjective authority."[2]

1 Jeffrey Stout, *The Flight from Authority: Religion, Morality, and the Quest for Autonomy* (Notre Dame: University of Notre Dame Press, 1981).

2 Bertrand Russell, *The Impact of Science on Society* (London: Allen and Unwin, 1952), 110–11; quoted in *Knowing and Being: Essays by Michael Polanyi*, ed. Marjorie Grene (Chicago: University of Chicago Press, 1969), 94.

Against the stream, as it were, and particularly against sentiments such as Russell's that would take authority as the enemy of science, truth, and human society, this book has endeavored to construct an extended justification of the claim that authority is necessary to us, particularly with an eye to the human good. We need the activity that authorities carry on in order to flourish as humans. Without authority, people cannot act in concert except in the least complex of situations, and in particular we would fail to achieve such complex projects as require the sustained, coordinated effort of humans over time. So human society requires authority. Likewise in human knowledge: we cannot maintain a culture of knowledge without authority, nor could we pass on the intellectual skills and insights that constitute a tradition without authority's ever-present activity. If we cannot have human society, much the more can we not have political society without authority. And if the church were to try to carry on without authority, it would cease to sing the chorales of God's praise, and the individual believers would then be unable to voice their confessions of faith—unable, that is, to bear and manifest their own authorization. Instead, a terrible centrifugal storm would set in, and believers would become like unmoored subatomic particles, shot randomly away from any center of intelligibility, and able to exist if at all for but a brief instant.

Let me work an analogy. Many people have wondered, given the fact that there is evil in the world, if there really could be a God. But suppose that we already have good grounds for concluding that God exists. Then the existence of evil is something to be held together with the existence of God, however paradoxical it may be; and our task is to seek how to hold the two claims together. This paradoxical path is, in my judgment, the only fruitful way we can approach "the problem of evil."[3]

Similarly, if we have good reasons to hold that authority is necessary for the flourishing of human beings, then the reality of evil in the form of fallible authority is not an argument against authority. It is, rather, a summons for us once again to see the paradoxical character of human existence. What then shall we do about the bind we are in, the peculiarly human bind?

The point requires emphasis. Demonstrably, on social, epistemological, political, and theological levels, in order to succeed as human

3 For an exemplary, recent book that takes this path, see Davies, *The Reality of God and the Problem of Evil.*

beings, *we need authority*; nonetheless, not only might authority willfully stray from its true purpose, *even if it is true* authority may still fail through the sheer finitude of human existence. Given this as our condition, what should we do? Should we "go with the flow" and try to live without authority? But that, if the analysis I have presented is correct, would be to live falsely. It would be to fail as human beings. What then can we do with this thing we need, this authority, which will never give us infallibly what we seek from it?

Our question might be put this way. Is there a way to live with fallible authority?

Illustration: The Rejection of Polanyi's Paper on Adsorption

Michael Polanyi showed us that the individual who seeks to know the truth—whether that individual be a judge, a researcher, an artisan, or whoever—must continue to live "convivially," which means in a society or with other seekers of truth in relationships characterized by being under authority. He also stressed our epistemological bind: authorities may prove to have been wrong. Nonetheless, Polanyi concluded that to reject authority would be to jettison culture, tradition, even knowledge itself; it would be a dear and costly act, devastatingly more costly than most people imagine. There is no getting around the hazard that what one holds as true may turn out to be false, even as the authorities of one's society (whether political or intellectual or even ecclesiastical) may turn out to have erred.

It is a conclusion to which Polanyi could give personal testimony, a conclusion for which Polanyi had, as it were, paid his dues. For early in his career Polanyi had had his scientific views rejected on the grounds that they ran against the then-established conclusions that scientists authoritatively accepted. The case involved Polanyi's development of a novel theory of adsorption (the phenomenon of the attachment of gas or other molecules to a surface). He published his theory in 1914. At first it seemed to be well-received. But other scientists were developing new theories of the construction of matter—theories that would undercut the basis of his theory of adsorption. Because of limitations of communication brought about by the war and the post-war upheavals in Hungary, Polanyi was unaware of these other developments. And so he carried on with experiments to prove his theory's validity.

At a decisive point he was invited to present his theory to a prestigious gathering of physical chemists; "Einstein," Polanyi writes, "was specially invited to attend my lecture." The result was of the sort that can sink a professional career: "Einstein and [Fritz] Haber decided I had displayed a total disregard for the scientifically established structure of matter."

Thanks only to his other contributions to the field was Polanyi able to maintain his standing as a physical chemist. He continued his labors in defense of his theory of adsorption. In 1930 Polanyi published a paper that, he thought, decisively refuted the objections that had been raised against his theory. But his paper was simply ignored. "It seems that by this time the opinion that my theory was false had hardened to a point where the reasons for which it had been rejected were forgotten." Only, it seems, in the 1950s was Polanyi's theory finally received as true.[4]

Ponder the significance of the charge that Polanyi had "displayed a total disregard" for something that was "scientifically established." The pressure of his intellectual peers was being applied to bring him into conformity with their recently settled conceptions. The epistemic authorities that are necessary for truth to be grasped were, in Polanyi's case, dismissing the views that he was advancing, and thus denying him authority—excluding him, we might say, from the web of epistemological authorization. In fact, as a professor, it was impossible for him to teach his own views, for the reason that his students had to pass exams that would be marked by others: they would be expected to know the conventional, "scientifically established" conclusions. And to teach his own views would presumably be, in addition, to put his students at a disadvantage on account of the time lost from the study of other matters.[5]

Altogether it was, as Polanyi wrote in 1963 with frankness, a "miscarriage of the scientific method." But such a miscarriage is also, in principle, unavoidable. Authorities cannot allow just any odd thing to be taught or published in academic journals, else the value of

4 His 1963 essay, "The Potential Theory of Adsorption," begins with the observation that in the 15 years since his turn from professional science to philosophy "occasional reports have reached me that my theory of adsorption, which hitherto had been rejected, was gradually gaining acceptance." Michael Polanyi, "The Potential Theory of Adsorption," in *Knowing and Being: Essays by Michael Polanyi*, 87–96; here 87. Quotations in the preceding two paragraphs are from 89 and 90.

5 See Polanyi, "The Potential Theory of Adsorption," 94.

the teaching or the journal be sunk under the weight of falsehood and sheer junk. Within a discipline there must be "discipline," and that "discipline" is what authorities command, and it is and must be "severe." Polanyi writes: "the scientific method is, and must be, disciplined by an orthodoxy which can permit only a limited degree of dissent, and...such dissent is fraught with grave risks to the dissenter. I demand a clear recognition of this situation for the sake of our intellectual honesty as scientists." They are deluded who, like Russell, picture science as an authority-free zone in which every pronouncement is evaluated afresh on the simple test of whether it accounts for the facts. On the contrary, science at any given time has an "orthodoxy" that can permit only a minimal amount of dissent. For "the authority of current scientific opinion is indispensable to the discipline of scientific institutions...its functions are invaluable, even though its dangers are an unceasing menace to scientific progress." And this authority of current scientific opinion is not expressed probabilistically; on the contrary, "I have seen no evidence that this authority is exercised without claim of certainty for its own teachings." The certainty that accompanies assertion, according to Polanyi, is the case unavoidably with personal knowledge in general, as we saw in Chapter 3. Human "commitment [by its very nature]...must go beyond the evidence."[6]

We should note it squarely. Polanyi's theory of adsorption was eventually seen to be true, even though he suffered its rejection and the possibility of the end of his scientific career for holding it earlier. But Polanyi does not conclude as a result that the scientific authorities—Einstein and the others—acted wrongly in upholding scientific orthodoxy. On the contrary, he says, it is necessary always to have an understanding of the truth of the matter at hand (here, physical chemistry), and there must be discipline to maintain and carry forth that culture, tradition, or body of knowledge. Such discipline cannot allow too much dissent. The scientific method miscarried in Polanyi's case, which is to say, it failed to separate the true from the false, and thus did not advance knowledge. But even when such miscarriages come home to oneself, one does not thereby achieve the right to deny the truth about the character of personal knowledge and thus about the character of authority; one does not thereby receive permission to undermine authority.

6 Polanyi, "The Potential Theory of Adsorption"; the quotations in this paragraph come from pages 92–4.

Embedded in Polanyi's reflections on his own case are the workings of a mature wisdom.[7]

What to do with the Fallibility of Authority

How then do we live with fallible authority? Not by a strategy of escape. That way is closed off to us, if indeed authority is necessary for our true human flourishing. Polanyi, as we just saw, emphasized the necessity of authority to science even as it is also a "menace" to scientific advance. We need continually to appreciate the weighty necessity of authority. There are good reasons for accepting authority as necessary in society, epistemology, politics, and the structures of the church. That authority, we have seen, always comes to us in persons who are authorities. And persons are limited, not only by sin, but by sheer finitude and the necessity to act in time. Nonetheless, the existence of error in the exercise of authority cannot argue for the elimination of authority.

Nor may we live and flourish with a strategy of undermining. This is the moral conclusion to draw from the model of wisdom that Polanyi gives us. Frustration with authority's errors is not license to subversion. To take the undermining way would be to act irresponsibly to the human call. Polanyi described his task in *Personal Knowledge* as an effort "to stabilize knowledge against scepticism, by including its hazardous character in the conditions of knowledge." Personal knowledge (which is any knowledge whatsoever) inevitably involves the passionate hazarding of a commitment that reaches beyond the evidence—beyond, that is, what can be said. The social "equivalent," Polanyi ventures, may be "in an allegiance to a manifestly imperfect society, based on the acknowledgment that our duty lies in the service of ideals which we cannot possibly achieve."[8] Polanyi was a scientist, and maintained his

7 This example from Polanyi's life shows, of course, the deep harmony between his reflections on his own experience and his explication of all knowledge as personal. Polanyi's student Richard Gelwick states: "Polanyi was led to the theory of tacit knowing, a theory that accounts for our personal participation in the finding and holding of knowledge. When we adequately understand this theory, we can see more clearly how a proper understanding of knowledge guides us to live within the bounds that we conceive to be true, but which might conceivably be false. This is a situation that calls for our acceptance of responsibility with no guarantee that we or our civilization will be right. It is a situation of hope acting on the confidence of our and others' universal intent." Gelwick, *The Way of Discovery*, 93.

8 *Personal Knowledge*, 245.

allegiance to scientific ideals despite their frustration in his case in the matter of adsorption. Every society, it seems to me, from an orchestra to an intellectual association to a fully political society and even the church: every society will fall short of its ideals. It will fall short, if for no other reason, because its authority will err, will be applied severely at times in error. Nonetheless, our duty, as Polanyi teaches by word and example, lies in our faithful continuance.

Still, our acceptance of the unavoidability of error does not mean we are reduced to passivity in the presence of such misfirings of authority. There is always tomorrow, and tomorrow, as Scarlett said, is another day. In an intellectual setting, the argument can continue to be made for the dissenting viewpoint (as Polanyi did, albeit without immediate effect). In politics there is the concept of a "loyal opposition." What "tomorrow" means is that even after authority has determined and executed a course of action, there are future days, future occasions, on which one may revisit the matter. The key is to do so faithfully, which is to say, without undermining the common good—without undermining authority itself.

One may loyally or faithfully accept the determinations of authority that one sees as erroneous, while at the same time one awaits appropriate opportunities to revisit the matter. To do so in no way undermines authority itself. For the very fact that authority itself is limited in time means that the actions authority takes, its determination of the means to achieve a common good, its material willing that the common good be brought about—these decisions and actions are themselves in time, and thus subject to time. No determination of authority can be the last word. Think back to an earlier illustration. An orchestra conductor may possess such authority that she is able to determine what music will be played, how it will be played, by whom it will be played, and even when it will be played. And the members of the orchestra will freely give their obedience to their conductor, because they recognize the good of common action that she makes possible for them. But the concert will come, the performance be given, the joy of it all had. And then it will be over. The orchestra gave their allegiance to the conductor for the sake of ideals that, inevitably, will have failed in some way fully to be achieved. And so there will be adjustments, conversations, perhaps realignments, and occasionally more drastic action. But even in the best case, there is something to learn, something new to incorporate into the old. Never does an orchestra conclude Beethoven's third symphony and *tout le monde* say, "That does it. No one ever needs to play that symphony again." And never does a good orchestra say,

"That does it. We are finished playing forever, and no orchestra will ever need to follow us."

But is it true that no determination of authority, of any sort, can be the last word? What of the case of intellectual judgments? Here the temporality of the determinations of authority may seem less clear. In intellectual judgments it is authority's role to assist in the apprehension of the truth about how things really are: and that truth, one would think, should partake of the permanence of its object. If the culture of scientific physical study has determined that gravity really is, precisely, an inverse-square law, this is a truth about the world; and unless gravity changes in the world, this truth will not change. Yet even here there is development of thought, as is well-known from many exciting scientific examples of the past few generations. We may succeed in apprehending a truth about the world, but we never apprehend the whole truth about the whole world. And we never will, for the fundamental reason that we are part of the world that we are trying to apprehend. So the determinations of intellectual authority, even in matters that might seem to be as rock-solid (if I may) as physics, always are made against a background of ignorance, the field yet to be studied which we can never grasp fully. And when something new is discovered—as happened with the discovery of transient subatomic particles—the new discovery causes a reevaluation of what we had already known, as we come to see it in a broader perspective, in a fuller light. It is still true that matter is made of atoms; yet we now know that atoms are, contrary to their name, not the tiniest subdivision of matter. We still have atoms; we still understand that things like water are composed of atoms in definite ratios; but the meaning of all that is complexified by the existence of proton, neutron, and electron (not to mention gluon and stickon, or whatever they're called).

What of judgments of right and wrong as given by an authority? Surely these require permanence, on account of a reason intrinsic to the nature of judgment itself. I have argued that the purpose of an authoritative judgment is achieved only by looking both backward and forward. As a declaration concerning what has been done, a judgment identifies where the fault lay in an action that is past. By doing so, and by declaring what shall be done about it, judgment puts an end to the past wrong and opens up the possibility of a new and liveable future for all parties. The conclusion would seem inescapable, that even if authority's judgments are temporal and transient elsewhere, here judgment needs fixity or else it simply won't accomplish its purpose.

And it is true that a particular judgment must be given fixity of a sort, or else through a never-ending process of appeals and reexaminations we would never get any judgments at all: and thus not have any common understanding of what has happened, and thus not have any way of moving forward. A single trespass would wipe out all social cohesion. Courts that are accomplishing their task have ways of assuring fair trials expeditiously conducted. For this reason, reviews of judgments, in many systems, are not permitted to reopen particular determinations, but are limited to considerations of wider applicability. There is nothing impossible about having a system wherein judgments when given are fixed and unappealable, yet not precedent-setting in themselves. The wider judgments of interlocking authorities could determine over time what counts as a valid precedent without undermining the fixity of the judgment given. Collective precedent would be an evolving body of judgment, fixed at any given time yet never complete, and in principle never complete-able.

So we can have the fixity of judgment we need in particulars, without entailing the permanence of that judgment as a determinative precedent. Let me push my argument to a limit. Even in theology, I say, the judgments of authority are fallible, in ways analogous to the fallibility of other forms of authority. I say this as a Christian of catholic conviction. I accept the enduring authority of Scripture as a finite and completed body of written text. I also accept the enduring authority of the Apostles' and Nicene Creeds. These are determinations of authority that cannot be gone back upon (without the church ceasing to be the church).[9] Nonetheless, since authority properly speaking is a performative concept, the authority of Scripture and creed is necessarily communicated humanly, in decisions and undertakings of persons who have and are under authority. And these decisions and undertakings cannot be intrinsically immutable, for they must be re-made, rearticulated, by living authorities again and again. New contexts, new questions, and advances in other fields of knowledge mean we ever await the fresh singing of a new aria.

All this should be sharply distinguished from an alternative means of dealing with the problem of fallible authority that might be a particularly American temptation. I refer to *the substitution of process and procedures* in the place of substantive determinations. Since authorities cannot guarantee that what they do will be infallible, perhaps we should not ask them to provide us with answers or judgments but

9 The church, that is to say, is indefectible.

rather with good procedures for the bringing about of answers and judgments. Thus certain elements in the American experience are taken to suggest that, given the fact that authority will err, we should pin our hopes on so structuring processes and procedures that the evils of error can be circumscribed or minimized. An American might think of Federalist paper number 10, wherein James Madison argues in favor of the United States Constitution that it has built-in structures to avoid the problem of rule by what he calls a "faction," a minority or majority that is able to push its own interest and does not rule with the good of the community at heart. We may remind ourselves of what these elaborate structures are in the 1787 text of the Constitution. To make a law according to that text requires a majority vote of the House of Representatives, each of whose members are directly elected by the voters in a specific district approximately equal in population to every other district; *plus* a majority vote in the Senate, whose members are elected by the legislatures of the various states and for a longer term, and who thus are more distant from popular passions, and who represent states and not equally-populated districts; *and* the signature of the President, who is elected by a college specifically called forth for the purpose, with the numbers of electors roughly proportionate to the population of the various states but slightly favoring the less-populous ones. One is aware, of course, that constitutional amendments, Supreme Court decisions, and technological advances in communication have conspired to lessen the strength of Madison's argument. It is much easier now for there to be a widespread passion of partisanship capable of enacting legislation without regard for the common good. But even the initial arrangement of checks and balances—the device adopted from Montesquieu to enable popular rule to rise above mob rule—was it not at best only a hope, and no guarantee? For let procedures be as complicated as we like, a determined group can co-opt those procedures to get its own way. This is bitter medicine for those who would think that the essence of authority is transparence and openness of procedure. They are destined to be saddened, if not shocked, as they find yet again that small-minded persons have found a way to game the system for themselves.

Yes, there may be procedures, checks and balances, which in a particular case are better than others. But no set of procedures will guarantee that authority will be preserved from error in its exercise. We are brought back to the human bind: the authority we need for our flourishing will also fall short.

My argument is that we must accept authority's substantive determinations, even when we are convinced they are wrong, but that this does not require us to *think* that they are right, nor does it silence us from responsible revisitations of the matter at hand, which, however, we must do in ways that do not undermine authority itself. Once we recognize that no particular structuring of authority will guarantee its right exercise, there is yet something to be gained in the attention to structure. Prudent action can be assisted by the intellectual tool that distinguishes between authority, which is necessary, and particular forms or structures of authority, which do not partake of the same necessity. I do not mean to suggest that all structurings of authority are indefinitely malleable. Nonetheless, the structures of authority, like its particular determinations, are not immutable. In particular circumstances, the development or change of those structures may be the course of wisdom. Let us think about these matters within our familiar four venues of authority, starting this time with the church.

Concrete Explorations of Fallible Authority

(1) The fallibility of church authority

The focal image of Chapter 5 was that of the individual believer rising from the congregation, supported by the structures of authority within the church, to be a listener to the Scriptures who now authoritatively "reads" the Scriptures in life. One such individual within the church is the theologian. And a way to ask the question of fallible authority is to ask what the relationship should be between the theologian (a particular sort of aria-singer) and the teaching authority carried out within and by means of the church's structures. What if the theologian comes to conclusions at odds with those of pope or bishop or synod?

We may take as culturally typical the views of a correspondent to the magazine *First Things*, published in response to a McGinley lecture that the Catholic theologian (and later Cardinal) Avery Dulles delivered at Fordham University. The correspondent characterizes Dulles's view as being that "theologians who do not satisfactorily toe the line" of the Catholic Church's magisterium contribute to the success of "the demonic power of a culture that refuses to submit to the discipline of faith." The author contrasts this view with one of free theological discussion unhindered by any church authority. While admitting the need "to identify and resist false theology," the author says that the means for doing so should be persuasion rather than coercion.[10]

What the author omits is something this book has shown before—for instance, in Chapter 4—that the supposed dichotomy of persuasion and coercion overlooks that which lies between the two, namely, authority. And since Dulles's original essay was titled "Teaching Authority in the Church," we may expect it to help us learn what to do with authority that is at once necessary and yet imperfect.

Dulles gives a brief account of the development of the functional distinction between the hierarchical magisterium of the Church and the work of theologians. In the early church, many bishops were also theologians. But the roles became specialized, so that today the word "magisterium" is applied more precisely to "the *public* teaching authority of the Church" held by "the class of people . . . institutionally empowered" to exercise it. Theologians, by contrast, are seen as "private persons in the Church" who cannot "speak for the Church as an institution." The teaching power of the hierarchy, its magisterium, is further to be distinguished from its judicial power. "Teaching is addressed to the intellect and calls for internal assent. Commands are addressed to the will and call for external obedience."[11]

This functional distinction, Dulles argues, is necessary. Scholars need freedom to pursue theological questions with the technical tools of their trade, and without pastoral burdens. The church's magisterium bears the pastoral burden, and thus needs to see that the teaching of the church is passed on clearly and intact. The two functions provide mutual assistance to one another. But on occasion there will arise conflict. How should conflict be handled?

Dulles urges theologians to have as their "first instinct" a desire "to accept and build on what is officially taught in the Church." The magisterium provides "a great benefit," so that even when theologians disagree with the magisterium, they should work so that their disagreement does not undermine its authority. In turn, the magisterium needs to value the services of theology, most of which "are positive" as "theology prepares the way for the magisterium to speak, and after it has spoken, theology explains and, as necessary, defends what has been

10 Letter to the editor, *First Things* no. 186 (October 2008): 14.

11 Avery Cardinal Dulles, "Teaching Authority in the Church," in *idem, Church and Society*, 18–19; emphasis original.

taught." These services require "freedom to follow the principles of their own special [theological] discipline."[12]

In practice, as Dulles admits, the magisterium may err (although, as a catholic theologian, Dulles also holds that it is possible for the church to speak infallibly, under certain precise conditions). In the period prior to Vatican II,

> several of the most eminent Catholic theologians, such as Henri de Lubac, Yves Congar, John Courtney Murray, and Karl Rahner, cautiously advocated doctrinal positions that were, for a time, resisted by the magisterium. They made their proposals without rancor and, when rebuffed, submitted without complaint.

These theologians were later rehabilitated, and proved to be highly influential theological experts in the course of the discussions at Vatican II. Dulles is unequivocal: "critical questioning of current magisterial teaching may sometimes be legitimate." If "some reformable teaching of the Church needs to be modified" or "the concepts that have been used for the communication of the faith are unsatisfactory in terms of contemporary science or knowledge" then "theologians have the right and even the duty to make their views known."[13]

On the other hand, there is also a manner of critical questioning that crosses over into illegitimacy. Dulles locates the problem in the attitude towards authority. Rather than accepting the need for authority, treating it with respect even when disagreeing with it, and accepting the decisions of authority when it pronounces against one's views (as was the example provided by de Lubac, Rahner, and others), this "criticism has been bitter and intemperate" producing "alienation."[14] Such criticism does not accept that the magisterium has the right to exercise discipline, even when (from the point of view of the critic) the magisterium is seen to be in error. In effect, this sort of dissent argues that persuasion alone can be accepted as authoritative.

In the Catholic Church, the magisterium exercises "a right of supervision over theology" so that dissent will not harm the church's faith and unity. The magisterium may: (1) require "prior censorship" on books of doctrine or liturgical texts; (2) require that articles and books for publication receive prior approval, the *imprimatur*; (3) control faculty appointments at seminaries and in licensed theological faculties;

12 Ibid., 21–2.
13 Ibid., 22–3.
14 Ibid., 22.

(4) warn against books that attack church doctrine.[15] This list, peculiar to the Catholic Church at this time, is neither exhaustive nor unchanging. I would argue that any institution, and certainly any church, must have some means for exercising authority over what is said in the name of that institution—even though what is said may on occasion turn out to have been wrong, if only in emphasis, or in lack of balance and nuance; still wrong and thus requiring future correction.

But there are things that the magisterium can and should do to prevent some conflicts, avoid some errors, and further the good for which the magisterium exists—the faith and unity of the church. Dulles identifies five such things. (1) The magisterium can be a moderating influence over opposing theological camps. Here its authority should be seen in its refusal, for instance, to countenance hasty charges of heresy. (2) It should restrain itself, and "avoid issuing too many statements, especially statements that appear to carry with them an obligation to assent." It is best for there to be as much freedom of doctrinal exploration as possible. (3) The magisterium should consult widely before it issues "any binding statement of doctrine." It is not helpful if the magisterium is seen to be isolated from ongoing theological discourse, or uninformed. (4) Objections to any proposed statement should be anticipated and addressed within the statement. (5) And the magisterium should be culturally sensitive in its pronouncements, something which it can achieve also by consultation in advance with representatives of differing cultures.[16]

In summary, Dulles shows the necessary dialectic between the institutional authority of the magisterium and the non-institutional authority of individual theologians. There needs to be a balance between the institutional teaching and disciplinary authority of the church, on the one hand, and activity of theologians who respect that authority while carrying out their own authorized task, even in times of conflict and, Dulles encourages, patient submission.

When we consider necessary institutional authority in the church—that which Dulles refers to in his Catholic context as the magisterium—we may find it helpful to bring to bear the distinction between the indispensability of authority and the changeability of its structures. In ecclesiological discussions, such a distinction can be found in many places, one of them being an Anglican document of ecumenical importance to which I now turn.

15 Ibid., 23.
16 Ibid., 24–5.

The Chicago-Lambeth Quadrilateral of 1886/88 is a document that purports to lay down the "inherent parts" of the "sacred deposit" of the church (so the General Convention of the Episcopal Church meeting in Chicago, 1886) or the "basis" for an "approach" to church reunion (so the Lambeth Conference of Anglican bishops, 1888). In the Quadrilateral, Anglicans insist that any reunited church have, in addition to the Scriptures, creeds, and the dominical sacraments of baptism and Eucharist, also the "Historic Episcopate." However, the Quadrilateral qualifies the historic episcopate with the words "locally adapted in the methods of its administration to the varying needs of the nations and peoples called of God into the Unity of His Church."[17] What might be permissible as a local adaptation is left unspecified. Bishops for a term only, who then cease to be such, as an adaptation to a democratic people (or to a historically German Lutheran people)? Bishops appointed by a secular official? Bishops elected by representatives of the laity? Bishops appointed by a pope? Such questions, exploring the field of "local adaptation," will have to be adjudicated in common meetings such as synods, conventions, and conferences. The point here is not to argue for the immutable necessity of a church having bishops, but rather to the foreseen necessity of (re)structuring the episcopal office in light of local conditions and emerging requirements.

Authority, we must keep reminding ourselves, is had and exercised by persons. In any structure there is a place (i.e., a person or persons) where binding decisions are made. As Anglicans of the "Liberal Catholic" school noted a century ago, there is nothing inherently wrong with the church taking on a papal structure—although they saw no inherent necessity for it either.[18] At times there may be need

17 The texts may be found in many places, one being the historical documents section of the 1979 Book of Common Prayer of the Episcopal Church, 876–8.

18 See, for instance, Wilfred L. Knox, "The Authority of the Church," in Edward Gordon Selwyn, ed., *Essays Catholic and Critical*, 3rd ed. (London: Society for Promoting Christian Knowledge, 1929). Knox argues for a theory of authority that incorporates the individual's undoubting acceptance "of the Catholic system" while recognizing that elements of that system may turn out to be erroneous. Knox says, with the pugnaciousness characteristic of the time, that there is no difference between his account of Anglo-Catholic belief on authority and "the most ultramontane theory" (114; see also 118–19). In the preface to the third edition, Selwyn urges that the truth about authority must include an account of its fallibility; that authority is more complex than advocates of "an infallible Pope, or an infallible Bible, or an infallible conscience" admit (vi). For a development of the similarities between this "Liberal Catholic" school and Polanyian epistemology, see Victor Lee Austin, "Is There an Anglican Method in Theology? Hints from the *Lux Mundi* Era," *Sewanee Theological Review* 42 (1999): 290–310.

for greater centralization, at other times decentralization; lay ministry may need to be encouraged, or excess enthusiasms may need to be channeled into the received patterns of orthodoxy.

(2) The fallibility of political authority

When a political authority errs, how may citizens respond? On the one hand, if the matter is neither large nor urgent, they may simply bide their time, enduring the error, waiting for opportunity, should it arise, for the judgment or law to be reversed. At the same time, they can make arguments for the wrongness of what political authority has done, but should do so as persons who are, and are seen to be, respectful and accepting of the political authorities. Responsible citizens can respond to the errors of political authority by making arguments, writing letters, donating money to advocacy organizations or political parties, and of course by voting. By sharp contrast, when the matter at hand (the injustice being committed or permitted by the political authority) is both great and urgent, persons may come to the reluctant conclusion that it is necessary to overthrow the existing political order using violent means. This is the most extreme case, the far-point on a spectrum of possibilities, and one concerning which serious persons have long had disagreement over whether in fact violent revolution can in any actual situation be justified. The argument against violent revolution hangs precisely on the necessity of authority to human flourishing. Thus those who engage in any violent revolution are under the obligation to manifest by word and deed that they are not attacking the notion of authority itself—that they are not anarchists. In his subtle analysis of this question, O'Donovan suggests that revolutionaries can prove their bona fides by showing that they wish to install a new governmental structure; and further, that they demonstrate their capability of doing so by their having a representative status even as revolutionaries.[19] However egregious the injustice, it is never enough to be, simply, against the status quo.

In cases of non-urgent matter, we should note the possibility that persons will come to discern, besides discreet occurrences of injustice, a *pattern* of misfirings of authority. Where there is a pattern of things going wrong, there is an argument for reshaping the structures

19 See Oliver O'Donovan, *The Just War Revisited* (Cambridge: Cambridge University Press, 2003), 64–77.

of authority. Discernment is required, and public discussion. There may need to be new courts, new superintendents, new laws or regulations, amendments to constitutions. No such change should be effected lightly or easily, but neither should it be impossibly hard to bring it about. An American rightly may be predisposed to see in his constitutional arrangements a salutary acknowledgment of the need for authority's structures to be adjusted continually under the press of events. It is hard to amend the U.S. Constitution, yet there is no provision in it that is unalterable.

Short of violent revolution, but stronger than the acceptance that accompanies continued attempts at persuasion (regarding both particular errors of authority as well as patterns of authority's failure), lies the significant response to misfirings of political authority that is known by the term "civil disobedience." The essence of civil disobedience lies in the conjunction of (a) the deliberate breaking of an unjust law with (b) the willful acceptance of the punishment for breaking that law. Classic examples in American history are the tax-refusal of Henry David Thoreau and the breaking of segregation laws by participants in the civil rights movement. The debates concerning the morality of civil disobedience pertain to its mediating character. On the one hand, if civil disobedience becomes too common or even fashionable, then it seems to trivialize the importance of persuasive argument. Not every error of authority should call forth an act of law-breaking, be the protestor ever so submissive to the arresting authorities. Civil disobedience is not a proper response to small matter. On the other hand, the insistence that proper civil disobedience accept the punishment of the law has led to the criticism that its practice may lend legitimacy to a regime that ought to be overthrown.[20]

The acceptance of the punishment of the law is the very public way whereby a citizen shows respect for political authority. The particular law that is broken in civil disobedience must be a law that is viewed as unjust. The argument must be, for instance, "It is wrong for the law to require segregation within the bus," or "It is wrong for the law to require payment of taxes that fund an unjust war," or "It is wrong for the law to permit persons to enter this building and perform abortions inside it." The law-breaker protests that the law is wrong, yet she does not go on to say, "And because the law is wrong, I should be allowed to violate it without consequence." Quite the contrary, by submitting

20 The classic study is James F. Childress, *Civil Disobedience and Political Obligation: A Study in Christian Social Ethics* (New Haven: Yale University Press, 1971).

herself to the authority of the state to exercise judgment upon her for breaking the law, the civil-disobedient lawbreaker recognizes the necessity of political authority.

In civil disobedience, as in the case of a theologian criticizing the magisterium, we can see at work an implicit authorization of the individual. Although political authority resides in authorized persons—magistrates, law-writers, police, judges of various sorts—there also resides within the individual the authorization to judge for herself the truth of the matter and how she should respond, when she judges that the political authorities have strayed into injustice. The authorization of the individual comes without coercive force. Yet it is hardly without effect, as examples from Mahatma Gandhi to Rosa Parks attest.

(3) The fallibility of epistemic authority

Epistemic authority, it would seem, presents the understanding with the most difficult cases. Political authorities who go astray do so with power, but not with truth; erring epistemic authorities, however, stray precisely with regard to truth. How to respond?

In Polanyi's case, detailed earlier in this chapter, the response was simply to persist as best he could, making arguments and presenting papers, within the accepted confines of the discipline. As it happens, Polanyi's developing interests in personal knowledge led him out of research chemistry; but there was no necessity for him to do so, and he could have continued in patience as a chemist to the end of his life.

There is no infallible method for determining that, in fact, an epistemic authority has made an error. If we could know *for sure* that an authority was wrong, we would be in possession ourselves of a purportedly infallible epistemic authority. But how could we know that we were infallible? Nonetheless a framework of understanding does seem to be able to present hints or suggestions that it is flawed (although they can never be more than hints or suggestions). Let me sketch a once-common pedagogical example.

Long ago, before there were satellites and GPS devices, sailors had to be able to tell where they were by using the stars. And they did so by using the understanding of the world—our universe—that had been laid down nearly two millennia ago by Ptolemy, the Egyptian astronomer, in his work *The Almagest.* And the basis of Ptolemy's system was that the earth was in the center of the world.

There are many tables in *The Almagest*, many complex calculations, many geometrical proofs; the English edition in the Great Books of the Western World series runs to nearly five hundred small-type two-column pages.[21] But let me give a vastly simplified account that will be adequate for our purposes. For illustration we take the planet Venus. Venus is imagined, first, to be moving in a perfect circle around the earth, because the circle is the perfect figure and the objects in the heavens are perfect objects. However, the appearance—the heavenly location—of Venus is different than this first calculation would give. So: an epicycle is imagined. An epicycle is a new circle whose center point moves around on the first circle. Instead of Venus moving around the earth, the epicycle moves around the earth, while Venus moves around the epicycle. Try this out: you'll see that by varying the size of the epicycle and the relative speeds, you can make Venus, from the point of view of the earth, move backwards sometimes (which, in fact, is what she is seen to do).

The matter is more complicated than I have made it—one needs another epicycle to get the data right, or (which gives the same result) an *equant* which makes the planet move equably on the circle around a point that is off-center. Such are the refined pleasures of working through Ptolemy.

But here is where the illustration becomes significant, and not merely antique. Suppose you are Copernicus looking at these Ptolemaic drawings. It may occur to you that there is one simple thing you can do, one change that will reduce the complexity of the system significantly. The change? Put the sun at the center, rather than the earth.

This is the standard story: Copernicus saw unnecessary complexity, and got rid of it by the simple change of putting the sun rather than the earth at the center of things. I believed this story myself, until I went back to look at the texts. It turns out that, although Copernicus complains of Ptolemy's unnecessary complexity, by the end Copernicus' system is itself just as complex.[22]

Yet Copernicus is able to give a *reason* for a feature that in Ptolemy's system was merely ad hoc. Of the planets, it is just Venus and Mercury

21 And this is only Books I–V of *The Almagest*. See *Ptolemy, Copernicus, Kepler*, vol. 16 of *Great Books of the Western World* (Chicago: Encyclopedia Britannica, 1952).

22 "The preface to [Copernicus'] *De Revolutionibus* opens with a forceful indictment of Ptolemaic astronomy for its inaccuracy, complexity, and inconsistency, yet before Copernicus' text closes, it has convicted itself of exactly the same shortcomings." Thomas S. Kuhn, *The Copernican Revolution: Planetary Astronomy in the Development of Western Thought* (Cambridge, Mass.: Harvard University Press, 1957), 171.

that are visible only when they are close to the horizon. Unlike the other planets, they never move beyond a certain limiting angular distance from the sun. Ptolemy has no reason to give for this. But when Copernicus makes Venus and Mercury inner planets, revolving like the earth around the sun but closer to the sun than the earth, then it is at once geometrically obvious why they never stray beyond a limit angle from the horizon. At the same time it is obvious why the other planets, being outer rather than inner, can appear in the sky at any distance from the horizon.

So we might say that Ptolemy's understanding of the world hinted at its fallibility, and the hint was this ad hoc feature of Venus and Mercury. Copernicus' system seems closer to the truth—Copernicus thereby claiming epistemic authority—because this new system has fewer arbitrary elements to it.

Unfortunately, the matter is not so simple. For Copernicus has created a problem that Ptolemy did not have. In Ptolemy, terrestrial and celestial objects are distinctly different kinds of things, with differing native motions. By nature, terrestrial objects move in straight lines. In contrast, celestial objects move by nature in circles. The problem that Copernicus has introduced is that he makes the earth act like a celestial object. How can this be? Why (in Copernicus) do earthly objects naturally move in straight lines while the earth itself, made up of those objects, naturally moves in a circle? It is a problem of physics unsolved in Copernicus—a suggestion within his own system that it too is not adequate to the truth about things. It will take Isaac Newton to resolve this tension—while introducing new tensions of his own.[23]

So while we are drawn to say that a simpler explanation, particularly one with fewer arbitrary features, is to be preferred, the reality of the history of thought seems to be that development and replacement of systems of understanding has proceeded with simultaneous increase and diminishment of complexity. Nonetheless, we do evaluate the judgments of epistemic authority with such criteria. Is the framework of understanding unnecessarily complicated? Does there seem to be an excess of arbitrary assumptions? Could this framework here, which deals with subject-matter X, be reconciled with that framework over there, which deals with subject-matter Y, resulting in a single framework that deals with both X and Y? In short, we look for simplicity of

23 I am grateful to Ron Mawby for drawing my attention to the simplifying and complexifying features of Copernicus' work.

concepts, breadth of application, and mutual interpretability, where the basic concepts illumine one another.[24]

There is no way to prove that the truth really is simple or unified; and no way to prove that a broader or less ad hoc framework of understanding is closer to the truth. We have to trust authorities, but authorities themselves are moved to grasp an understanding that goes beyond proof.

Thus we must deal with misfirings of epistemic authority by acknowledging the necessity of that authority, while at the same time probing whether existing authoritative understandings are in fact leading us towards the truth, recognizing, however, that our "probing," while generally seeking simplicity and unity of comprehension, nevertheless can follow no definitive method.

(4) The fallibility of social authority

Before we considered God or power or truth, there was the basic fact of human sociality: the human being desires goods that are not individual but common, and that basic fact about us was the first occasion for us to see the necessity of authority. Through a variety of societies, in a complex web of overlappings and incorporatings, human beings fulfill who they are by the achievement of human goods each one of which is beyond the reach of an individual acting alone. The thesis of Yves Simon, to which this book has often reverted, is that in any society authority is essential to make determinations about the means to achieve the common good, and it is further most essential to provide the ongoing willing of the matter of that common good. What then shall we say of this most basic form of authority, social authority, if it errs and strays from its purpose?

Say you are the oboist in your city's symphony orchestra. Your conductor is enforcing idiosyncratic interpretations of the music you are playing this season. Your sense is that the result is displeasing to the refined audience that you hope the symphony is cultivating.

24 Here I should note again the important work of Thomas Kuhn, who, as I mentioned in Chapter 3, bequeathed to our discourse the terms "paradigm" and "paradigm shift." The accumulation of data alone cannot account for a revolution in our understanding of reality. Scientists, Kuhn says, do not operate as naive, ahistorical fact-gatherers who then deduce theories. Polanyi's point regarding personal knowledge, of course, is that no one operates that way.

Furthermore, from a personal standpoint, you feel that her interpretation makes the oboe lines particularly unpleasant; rather than contributing to a harmonious texture of sound, your performance under her direction is jarring and off-putting. In short, in these particular ways, your conductor is impeding the accomplishment of the common good; she has authority, but she is not using it well. What can you do?

One thing you might do is grumble. You could gossip with the other instrumentalists about the conductor's failings. You could engage in strategies of low-grade subversion: arriving late, or putting butter on the handle of her car. You could speak, anonymously, to a reporter at your local newspaper. You could try to make the rest of the orchestra, and such audience as attends, as unhappy as you are. And although you might say the contrary to yourself, you would be doing these things because you had ceased to care about the common good.

"My way or the highway" is what it's called. Its tools are grumbling, gossiping, back-biting, and an almost infinite resourcefulness to the multitudinous, quotidian forms of a serious spiritual malady. The malady is pride, and for pride I now give this book's definition. Pride is the refusal to acknowledge our need for authority. And pride is working its trouble everywhere.

There is another way, but I must tell you it has the hardness of ascesis. You might go to the conductor directly with your complaints. You would need to demonstrate your bona fides, that you truly cared for the common good, the purpose of the orchestra. Such demonstration entails an acknowledgment of and appreciation for the authority of the conductor. And if the conductor refused to listen to you? There might be other appropriate actions for you to take, depending on circumstances. But face it squarely: there may come a time when there is nothing else that you can do *without compromising the ability of the orchestra to achieve its common good.* This is the hard ascesis of self-denial: it may be necessary for such achievement of the common good as is possible, that you silently bear with—even cheerfully and silently bear with—the wrongly-exercised authority of your conductor. At least, you are not being subjected to physical abuse; your views on musical interpretation, while probably correct, may still not be so; if over time your views do not change you can give appropriate notice so that you can leave the orchestra without unduly harming it. So you do have options.

But let us not back away from the truth. At times, the human good requires that we submit to social authority that we believe is wrong.

Why is this so hard to do? Why is our pride particularly defined by our resistance to the necessity of authority?

The answer has been told in a thousand stories. Once long ago our first parents were given life and language and love. They lived in innocent harmony with themselves and their maker. But they did not want to live in harmony: they preferred isolation over communion. So they broke with their creator, and they started breaking with each other. In one such story, the first generation rebels against God, and in the second generation fratricide enters the world.[25]

If I am right to characterize sin as the choice of isolation over communion, then it follows that sin amounts to a rejection of the essential social character of human beings. It should be no surprise, then, that we have trouble with authority, for authority is a reminder built into our world that we cannot make ourselves. We are not proud and princely individuals, endowed with primordial independence, who then concede authority as a matter of self-decision.

Sin is the reason authority strikes us so hard, but sin is not the reason we need authority. Authority points to what is true about human beings in their best condition, as full and complete beings living in friendship with one another—about which I will say more in the final chapter.

Let me home in on this destructive aspect of the rejection of authority. As a priest, I have seen it everywhere, but it doesn't take peculiarly priestly eyes to do so. A person arrives at church and finds that a visitor is sitting in "his" pew. So he gives her a nasty look, and sits right behind her. He grumbles to his friend beside him, in a voice intended to be heard by the stranger, that he doesn't understand why people come to this church who don't understand what's going on. He sings with a voice he intends to be obnoxious. He gives a running critical commentary on the visitor. You think I'm exaggerating? You imagine that church people are always glad to have visitors? Friend, I wish you were correct. But the church-person I here describe is real—he is Legion—and he would plainly prefer the destruction of the common good for which the church exists rather than accede to the church authorities who allow strangers to sit in his seat!

I know I am not exaggerating, because I have seen such in myself. A decision is made by an authority that strikes me as a wrong decision, and I will secretly hope (to my shame) that the whole enterprise goes down. "If it's not going to be done my way, well, let the thing

25 See Gen. 3–4.

fail; I don't care." What is a "passive-aggressive" person if not one who resents authority?

A decline in social vibrancy or cultural texture, an increase in social problems: these are some of the consequences of our rebellion against authority. Our rebellion weakens the symphony, the neighborhood, the company, the household, with the result that we live with less social texture than we might have had. Yet there are always positive things we can do. Our concern is not only to do the best we can with the authorities we have, but also to foster new mini-societies, new structures of authority, to fill social needs. Much good is achieved this way, often quiet and unnoticed, and yet essential to human flourishing. Visionary individuals see the need for a new youth music organization, for instance, and they bring it about. Neighbors see the need to organize to keep their street's walls clean of graffiti. Entrepreneurs see the possibility of bringing jobs to an economically depressed area, and they identify the needed factors for those jobs to materialize.[26] Here social authority grows and with it a rejuvenation of the human world.

26 For a remarkable account of an entrepreneur working on social and political systems to help people move out of poverty, see Gary MacDougal's memoir, *Make a Difference* (New York: St. Martin's Press, 2005). Also remarkable, with an international focus, is Jacqueline Novogratz, *The Blue Sweater: Bridging the Gap Between Rich and Poor in an Interconnected World* (New York: Rodale Books, 2009).

Chapter 7

CONCLUSION: AUTHORITY IN PARADISE

Authority Without Compulsion

It is not sin that makes authority necessary (so this book has argued); rather, even if human beings were unencumbered by sin they would still need authority in order to flourish. In particular, apart from any considerations of sinfulness, both social authority and epistemic authority are necessary to human flourishing. Political authority is somewhat different, as I have argued, in that, apart from sin, its element of coercion would not be necessary. Still there would be a need for political authority to provide social authority at the level that includes the entire political community, the judgments that enable a community to will and to achieve large-scale common goods.

But what then might we think about the place of authority at the end of it all? When governments pass away, and their for-the-time-being provision of judgment reverts to the Judge of all; when the institutions and practices of the church pass away, as that which they have anticipated, foretold, and made sacramentally present becomes fully real—what then is the point of authority? Does authority have a place, so to speak, in heaven? Is there truly no contradiction between the notions of "paradise" and "authority?" In the Christian understanding, is authority something that humans need *all the way*, "world without end"?

To speak of heaven is to wade into a cultural morass. Many people seem to be willing to believe anything at all about heaven, provided that what they believe gives comfort. So, at the time of death, the thought is widely voiced that the real person has not died. Aunt Marge, one might say, has been released from her suffering. She is not dead; she has "passed away." One might even speak of Aunt Marge looking down upon her funeral proceedings (sorry, the "memorial service") with benevolent smile. So the deceased person is imagined to continue forever in a bodiless existence, perhaps very close to earth, spirit-like, an ongoing near-participant in our everyday life. Again, to anyone who thinks I overstate the matter, ask a priest about the difficulty we have in naming the liturgy correctly. There are many people who recoil at the very mention of the word "death," many who prefer that the liturgy be called "A Thanksgiving for the Life of Marge Smith." But what is the correct title of this service? At least for Anglicans, it is this: "The Burial of the Dead."[1]

Christians believe people die. Because a human being is body and soul together, there can be no human being when there is no living body. But for Christians, the death of a person is not the last thing to be said about her. The Christian hope includes an expectation of a personal and general resurrection, when all persons are raised to be judged by Christ, who will come "to judge the living and the dead," as the Creed has it.[2] Of the interim time, between death now and resurrection then, it is impossible positively to state anything, except that whatever is said about the in-between state must not deny (1) the anthropological claim that a human being is an ensouled body, not a soul trapped in a body; and (2) the eschatological claim that there will be a resurrection at which time real human beings (i.e., not bodiless souls) will be judged.[3] Yet whatever else happens following death, this happens: a resurrection of all to a judgment that is on each.

At that judgment, some, at least, will be invited to enter the joy of the Lord. They may be surprised at the outcome; "Lord, when saw we thee an hungred, and fed thee?" (Mt. 25.37). Many a cautionary tale

1 So in the 1979 U.S. Book of Common Prayer; in the first Prayer Book of 1548/49: "The Ordre for the Buriall of the Dead." For an analysis of late-modern interpretations of death, afterlife, and heaven, as well as a vigorous re-presentation of the traditional Christian view, see N. T. Wright, *Surprised by Hope: Rethinking Heaven, the Resurrection, and the Mission of the Church* (New York: HarperOne, 2008).

2 For this phrase, the language of the Apostles' and Nicene Creeds is identical.

3 Besides N. T. Wright, mentioned above, another masterful account of the tradition, itself open to new understandings consistent with the tradition while developing it in interesting ways in the light of theological research, is Joseph Ratzinger, *Eschatology: Death and Eternal Life*, trans. Michael Waldstein and Aidan Nichols (Washington, D.C.: Catholic University of America Press, 1988).

has told us that we may be surprised at *who else* is there.[4] Yet whoever they are, and whatever their number, and even whether we are among them: these are questions we may lay aside for the purposes of this book. It is enough for us that the set is not empty. There are (or, at least, there are to be) persons in heaven,[5] persons who enjoy the Lord for ever.

The question is this. For human beings who have been raised from the dead and thus are really human (with body and soul), and are fully human (without the subtraction of sin), and who enjoy heaven—is authority still a function within their social reality? Such persons have been referred to in the tradition as the redeemed, the saints in light, the blessed ones in glory, those who see God face to face. And my question is, how can we understand authority as something still with them?

Dante's Ordered Spheres: Ranking that is Neither Higher Nor Lower

The problem seems to stem from our inability to imagine people in heaven as having intrinsic differences. Yet if there is authority in heaven, then there will have to be differences. There will be those in authority, and those under authority. And the fact that anyone in authority is also himself under authority does not mitigate the problem of the inequality. Moreover, if there is authority, there are those whose responsibility, under authority, is to listen and to act in accordance with what they hear. In the next section of this chapter I will expand on the notion that decisions are made in heaven; I will argue that since heaven is an active community in which decisions are made, it is ever more interesting and creative, and that the interest and creativity are possible thanks to the persistence of authority in heaven. But first we must get out of the way the sense that any difference of the sort that authority entails is incompatible with the equality we expect in heaven. I put it bluntly. If heaven is the enjoyment of the

4 The Big Man in C. S. Lewis's "dream" *The Great Divorce* is shocked that a murderer has come from heaven to greet him. C. S. Lewis, *The Great Divorce* (New York: Macmillan, 1946; repr. New York: HarperCollins, 2001), chapter 4.

5 I speak of "in heaven" for convenience only. I mean, more precisely, persons in the post-resurrection state who enjoy the Lord, that is the presence of God (as I develop more fully below). Whether that is what the biblical tradition means, or what we ought to mean, by the term "heaven," is not at stake in this usage.

Lord, could one person enjoy the Lord more than another? And if so, could the other really be happy? And if he is not happy, then he is not flourishing (since happiness at its most essential level, as Aristotle told us, is living as an excellent human being, that is, flourishing), and if he is not flourishing, he cannot be in heaven. Another way of putting this is to say that José may be perfectly happy that Rosie is different from him, but if Rosie is (eternally, forever) in authority over him, even if Rosie is also under others' authority, José will feel himself less than perfectly happy. For we moderns have rejected the idea that happiness is found in our accepting our rank and place in a hierarchical world. If one must be submissive to be happy in heaven, is one truly happy?

The pilgrim of the year 1300, the character "Dante" in the *Divine Comedy* written by Dante, finds otherwise when he makes his journey to heaven. He finds intrinsic differences that do not mean differences in delight, and that do not entail any greater distance from the Lord. Follow me.

Dante's journey is in three parts. The first part requires that he descend from the surface of the earth to its center; this is the trip through hell, at the end of which, at the very center of the earth (which is the geographical center of the universe), he sees Satan frozen in ice. The second part of his journey is then an ascent, a briefly-told rising to the far surface of the earth to a land no one can reach this side of death, whence he climbs the mountain of purgation. In the final part of his journey, Dante is taken up from the top of that mountain, which is the earthly paradise, and is carried through space until at the end he beholds the vision of God.

His paradisiacal journey takes him through several heavenly spheres—the spheres within which move the moon, the planets and the sun, the fixed stars, and finally the fixed crystalline sphere that surrounds all.[6] In each of these spheres he meets some of the people who are in paradise. Finally he is taken "beyond" the outermost sphere, and he enters the empyrean, where Dante the author pulls upon us something like a geometrical slight of hand.

For the empyrean is a stadium, and the real dwelling place of all the saints is there, not in the spheres through which Dante has passed. The saints in the empyrean are forever in the presence of God, in love, with the Triune Reality in their very center. It was only out of

6 For a map and outline, see Dante Alighieri, *Paradiso*, trans. Robert and Jean Hollander (New York: Doubleday, 2007), xxvi–xxvii.

condescension for Dante, because he would not be able to understand the empyrean, that the saints moved out into the various spheres. In fact, it was something like a cosmic command performance, all for his sake; and as soon as Dante had met them, they returned to their true home, the presence of God.

I say this is "like a geometrical slight of hand" because it entails a transformation of what is the center of the universe. From the beginning of the journey, Dante has been exploring the world, first descending to the pit at the center, and then rising outward through purgatory and through the ever-larger spheres of "paradise." But at the very end, the universe is transformed, turned inside-out as it were; Dante passes through the outermost sphere and finds that he is, only now, moving toward the center; the center turns out to be the Triune God.

We might think of it the following way, although Dante, on my reading, doesn't go so far. While Dante the character is ascending through the heavens, moving from sphere to sphere and, in the various spheres, meeting and speaking with and learning from a number of saints, it turns out that these spheres, instead of getting ever larger as Dante travels further out, are instead reversely concentric, so that Dante, instead of moving away from the center of the earth, instead moves towards the center of the heavenly spheres. We have permission, as it were, to conceive things this way, since the saints in those various spheres are really not there but in the empyrean, concentric about God himself. Instead of moving from earth outwards and upwards to ever-vaster spheres of heaven, Dante moves through spheres that are nested, each one *inside* its predecessor (not outside), and he is closing in, ultimately, on the vision of the Triune Being of God, the focal point at the center of paradise.

And this transformation of reality is *a categorical subversion of static hierarchies.* Thereafter, differences in rank are not causes of sadness (or even shame) but rather sources of joy. Dante learns this in the first sphere, that of the moon, when he meets the nun Piccarda. She tells him that although, because she neglected her vows, she is placed in the slowest sphere—the furthest sphere in paradise from God—nonetheless she is blessed. Dante wonders at this; do she and her companions not desire "a more lofty place, to see more, or to make yourselves more dear?" (III.65f.).[7] She answers with smiles and

7 Here and after, quotations are from *Paradiso,* trans. P. H. Wicksteed (London: J. M. Dent and Sons, 1965). Canto and line numbers are given parenthetically in the text.

gladness, as if she were burning with "love's first flame" (69), and her first word is to address Dante as *Frate,* "Brother" (70). She states that everyone's desire in heaven is to do the will of the one who assigns places to all of them—and her address of Dante as brother is itself a sign of the harmonious love of all for all. Thus the rank or place that each one has, "from threshold unto threshold throughout the realm, is a joy to all the realm" (82f.). The rank of everyone pleases everyone; it is joy within joy upon joy. In short: "his will is our peace" (85). At once Dante understands: "everywhere in heaven is Paradise, e'en though the grace of the chief Good does not pour down there after one only fashion" (88–90).

And yet, is this answer sufficient for us? There seems to be the following problem: it leaves Piccarda in the sphere of the moon, at the farthest remove in paradise from God, as if she were only granted a lawn ticket to a concert, content to listen to the music through electronic speakers, unable to obtain admission to get close to the live performance. Thus the importance of what I've already mentioned, the fact that these saints that Dante meets in the various spheres, of which saints Piccarda is the first, are not truly where Dante sees them. Beatrice, Dante's guide, enlightens him. In truth, she says, all the souls in paradise are together, and none has a bliss that lasts "more [or] fewer years." No, "all make beauteous the first circle," all share the "sweet life," *dolce vita* (IV.33–35). Nonetheless, there are distinctions according to their ability to respond to the Holy Spirit, "feeling more and less the eternal breath" (36). Robert Hollander, in his note to this line, suggests we think of "professionals who gladly admire the greater ability of their betters and enjoy participation in the same activity in which these 'stars' excel."[8] And that is indeed a helpful suggestion, pointing to a hint in our present life of the quality of the joys of the life to come. Yet we must not forget the geometrical inversion of the passage to the empyrean itself, the subversion of static hierarchies. The joy of heaven is not admiration at any distance. The intrinsic differences in paradise are had by persons who are in close solidarity, so much so that the joy of each is the joy of all.

Still the solidarity, the communion of love around the Trinity, does not erase the differences. So, Dante would show us, the notion of authority is not antithetical to the notion of paradise.

8 Dante, *Paradiso,* trans. Hollander, 98.

Authority in God

Authority is not something we need to grow out of, because authority is part of our being all the way to the end, "world without end." When we have reached the empyrean, the true center of the universe, we have come to the presence of God, to the state of being where we see God directly, as he is (see 1 Cor. 13.12). And the truth about God is that he is not a monad, but a Trinity of Persons. Here we come to mysteries that are beyond the power of speech to comprehend, as Dante, all but speechless, tells us at the end of *Paradiso*. T. S. Eliot spoke of the Incarnation, the Christian doctrine cognate to that of the Trinity, that the contemplation of it was an occupation that only a saint could undertake. And even then, what was possible was at best "to apprehend" the point where God entered and took on time.[9] To "comprehend" would be to get your prehensiles around, that is, to embrace or surround or, as we say, to grasp with your understanding. To apprehend, by contrast, is but to touch; it is not to surround or grasp but only to make a sort of contact. With regard to the deep mysteries of God's being, the very best even a saint can do is to achieve a limited apprehension. There's no comprehending of God. One might note that "the darkness," referred to in the opening of St. John's Gospel, is said never to have been able to "comprehend" the light of the Incarnate Word; a modern translation nicely captures the point when it says, "the darkness has never mastered [the light]."[10] There's no mastering of God, not by anyone, although (unlike the darkness) we need not fight against him.

Without pretensions to sanctity, let us nevertheless make bold to take up the occupation of a saint and attempt to apprehend the import of the Trinity, the remarkable datum of faith that the center of the universe's praise is no monad. Here at the threshold of the empyrean I attempt to say a few things that go beyond what I said at the end of Chapter 5, when speaking about authority in the church.

In the creedal language, we speak of Father, Son, and Holy Spirit.[11] The Father has priority; it is from him that the Son and Spirit proceed.

9 T. S. Eliot, "The Dry Salvages," line 200, in *Four Quartets* (New York: Harcourt Brace Jovanovich, 1971).

10 So the *New English Bible* (New York: Oxford University Press, 1971), Jn 1.5.

11 Here I follow what is called the Nicene Creed in generally-accepted English translation.

Of them, the Son is spoken of first: he is "begotten" of the Father "eternally." But this procession of the Son does not make the Son any less than the Father. The Son is God, light, true God, and indeed "of one Being" with the Father. Similarly, although the Spirit proceeds from the Father,[12] he is no less God than either the Father or the Son; together with them, he is worshiped and glorified.

So we have three "Persons" amongst whom there is the ranking of priority (the Father comes first, however we rank Son and Spirit) and yet who differ not at all from each other with regard to "substance" or "being." Each is, full stop, "God," not "a god."[13] This leads to many problems of understanding; in fact, this is why comprehension of God is impossible. For us and other material beings, we can have different individuals with the same substance (understood as "nature" or "essence" or "kind of thing") because those different individuals have different matter. Matter, as Aquinas would say, is an individuating principle. But there is no matter in God. And that's just one of the many problems in the way of understanding God.

The way to begin to apprehend the truth about God is to speak of the Trinity not as three individuals but as three relations. Theology often suggests we take each of the Persons as a "subsisting relation," which is an oxymoron, since relations are properties that things have: I am the reader of this book; the writing table is in front of me; and so forth. "Readership" and "in front of" are relations that things like books, readers, and tables can have; which is to say, relations are derivative realities that rely upon preexisting substances. There's no "reading" without substantive readers to do it. In our experience, indeed in our language, relations don't just exist. Nonetheless, and despite its unimaginability, "subsisting relation" points us toward the truth about God and away from certain common errors. To be the Son *is nothing else than* to be the Son of this Father; to be the Father *is nothing else than* to be Father of this Son; to be the Spirit *is nothing else than* to be the Spirit of this Father (and this Son), the joy or love or will that God

12 Or "from the Father and the Son," or "from the Father through the Son." The resolution of the *filioque* controversy, while much to be desired on grounds ecumenical and evangelical, will not affect the general claim here made about difference and authority within the Trinity.

13 The "gods," of course, are not really "God," because they are beings within the universe of creation, existing alongside other beings like corn-plants and pigs and people. "God" is not a member of a class; for that reason, although there can be no other God, it can be misleading to speak of God as "one." As noted earlier, McCabe puts the paradox thus: God plus the universe cannot make two. See *God Matters,* 6.

has (and which, as we said in Chapter 5, must be God). That is to say, there is nothing to the Son that makes him different from the Father other than the given reality that he is the Son of this Father. He is—his identity is nothing but—the relation; he is a subsisting relation.

There is authority being exercised here, in the very being of the Triune God, which I will try to show by speaking now about the Incarnation. Herbert McCabe would use the image of a film projector to get at what is going on in the Incarnation. A film projector—there may be readers too young to have ever seen one—is a machine that shines light through successive frames of transparent film. The light is projected onto a screen, and there you see what is called, by analogy, the "film." McCabe often said that the Incarnation was God's own life, the life of Father, Son, and Holy Spirit, being projected onto the screen of human history.[14] The Incarnation is God's life made visible to us, but visible within the world of sin that we humans have made, which made it inevitable that Jesus would die.

Thus when we see the life of Jesus we see the life of God, subject to the distortions made upon it by sinful human history. In the creedal language, it is the Son of God who takes on flesh (*carnis*) and is made man. When we see Jesus we behold that second subsisting relation of the Trinity, the Son who is begotten eternally by his Father. Of course, since the Son is of one Being with the Father, and has no substantial difference from the Father (his only difference is that he is the Son to this Father), then when we see Jesus we are seeing God. As I've said before, statements like "God ate a fig and enjoyed it" are literally true (on the assumption that at some time Jesus ate a fig and enjoyed it; once he famously didn't [Mt. 21.19]).

So let us think about Jesus' obedience. Obedience, recall, has to do with listening and acting accordingly. Jesus states that what he has heard from the Father is what he has spoken. Jesus is true to his Father. He does his Father's will and refuses to allow himself to be deflected from it. Sin in the world offers the occasion for Jesus to consider the possibility of having a will that is different from his Father's. Thus does the devil tempt him at the beginning of his ministry; thus, at the end, does he face the prospect of his excruciating death. But he is obedient: "nevertheless not my will, but thine, be done" (Lk. 22.42). From beginning to last he holds his Father's will as his own.

14 See, for example, *God Matters*, 22: "The story of Jesus is what the eternal trinitarian life of God looks like when it is projected upon the screen of history."

Which is to say, the Incarnation as the story of God projected upon human history shows that the Father has authority over the Son. Indeed, in the strongest terms, the identity of the Son is inseparable from the authority of the Father over him. "I and my Father are one" (Jn 10.30). And yet: this complete obedience (complete listening) to the Father has the outcome in human history that is more surprising than any other thing that has ever happened. Hear Saint Paul tell the story. The Son was "obedient unto death, even the death of the cross. *Wherefore* God also hath highly exalted him, and given him a name which is above every name: that at the name of Jesus every knee should bow...every tongue should confess..." (Phil. 2.8–11; emphasis added). Jesus' obedience is the causal condition—"wherefore"—that leads to Jesus' exaltation. In this book I have often adverted to the story of the centurion whose servant was ill (Mt. 8.5–10). To that centurion it was given, we may now say, to experience the projection of the life of the Trinity upon human history. For he saw that Jesus' authority came from Jesus' own obedient submission to the one over him. The Son's authority comes from his eternal, obedient submission to the Father. Authority is the structure of reality: to have it is to be under it. Jesus' resurrection also shows the converse: truly to be under authority is to be lifted into authority. The Father eternally bestows himself upon the Son.

It is to that dynamic movement that consideration of the Trinity drives us. Authority is not static, but flows through the movements of listening and acting accordingly and being raised—the movements of humility and exaltation, both of which can be misunderstood and yet both of which are essential, not first of all to us, but to God. The key point is that the divine Persons have no difference in substance. As subsisting relations, they lack any antecedent identity into which they might revert and rest. God is dynamic all the way down. We might possibly think about ourselves, that we could work diligently and faithfully and make something of our lives...and then retire, rest, stop our labors, repose in the substance that is who we are. We would be mistaken, but we can understand our mistake. It's the same mistake as thinking that to have authority is a static and uni-dimensional reality, the mistake of thinking of authority as meaning, with no remainder, "authority over." It is not so. Lacking individual substance, the divine Persons can only rest and repose in their dynamism. This is paradoxical speech, the paradox of relations that subsist in no antecedent being.

Our Being in God

Why did I just now say that there is no rest, that it is a mistake to think we labor and then, at the end, get to repose in the fruits of our labor? Robert W. Jenson has a thin book with a modest subtitle, "Resolutions of Difficult Notions." The book, *Thinking the Human*, explores persistent conundrums of human existence such as death, consciousness, freedom, and love. Jenson says that we customarily think that we know very well what it is to be human, but that understanding God is the problem. Yet when we try to think about death, consciousness, and so forth, we discover that what it is to be human is also eluding our comprehension. In this dense, insightful book, Jenson takes each conundrum and shows how it can be resolved if only we take the Christian doctrine of the Trinity seriously. In other words, both God and the human are beyond our comprehension; yet, apprehension (in the sense discussed above) of the one can lead to apprehension of the other.[15]

So the last thing I want to say in this book is this. The dynamism of the life of God, which we see in the authority obeyed and bestowed, which is inseparable from the identity of the divine Persons—this dynamism also belongs to human persons, and characterizes us eternally. We will never rest in ourselves. And that is good news.

Authority perdures among human beings to the end. Freed of sin, human beings in paradise are liberated from such things as jealousy, small-mindedness, and hatred. The lack of sin means an increase of human capacity, for sin is always a diminishment of the human, a reduction of what we are able to do. No place in the universe is as small as hell, as C. S. Lewis showed memorably towards the end of *The Great Divorce* when his character George MacDonald reaches to a tiny gap in the soil between two blades of grass and says that all of hell could be contained there.[16] No place in the universe is as frozen, as lifeless, as the pit of hell, as Dante saw when he got there: it was ice, not fire; rigidity, the death of all activity. Paradise, by contrast, is the place of true activity. Philosophers have intuited such every time, following Aristotle, they have described God as "pure act." But this insight needs to be taken with complete trinitarian seriousness. I have spoken already of

15 Robert W. Jenson, *Thinking the Human: Resolutions of Difficult Notions* (Grand Rapids, Mich.: Eerdmans, 2003).

16 Lewis, *The Great Divorce*, 137–8.

the essential dynamism of God's triune being. Essential activity marks also the being of the blessed.

For we are creatures who speak with one another. Speaking, we are able to speak about things that are and about things that are not; we can speak *modally*, of things that might be, or perhaps should be, or might be in this way or that; we can speak about various possibilities and how we might bring them about. Speaking, we can work together towards the achievement of new projects, without end.

This is the essential creativity of human beings, a creativity that in heaven explodes beyond all the bounds of sin and death. Think again of music, of our hypothetical orchestra that has been with us for so much of this book. There is always new music in heaven, and it rises continuously without any concomitant loss of portions of the old. More music is composed, more instruments created, more variations and improvisations upon harmonic structures and thematic overlays. Heaven is an on-going explosion of music, whose variety and texture and delightfulness increases exponentially without end. It bursts all imagining.

And with each increase of complexity, there are more decisions to be made. There is more music to choose from: which composition shall we play now? There are more instruments we might use: which ones shall we use today? There are even more legitimate interpretations, since each variation of interpretation evokes resonances with the expanding creative universe: what shall be our interpretation today? None of these decisions can be reached by reason alone, since reason itself is expanding as the reality which it strives to understand—the music of heaven, in this case—is also expanding. Decisions must be made; reason alone cannot yield them; how are the decisions to be made?

They are made joyfully by authority. Heaven is a state of activity of people who are undiminished by sin, whose activities will have to be decided upon, which decisions entail the ongoing provision of authority. This is not authority that partakes of coercion, as must political authority as we know it today. It is simply social and epistemic authority, exercised by redeemed persons over redeemed persons and under redeemed persons, for the joy of all.

I think we can see its dynamic by reference to the authority of the Son. He was obedient to death, and therefore given the highest authority. Redeemed persons in Christ have also died and risen in promise (as Paul says; see Rom. 6.3f.). By the grace of the Holy Spirit, they have entered into the obedience of the Son to the Father. They thereby died to sin and were raised to new life. These eschatological events that are bestowed in the sacrament of baptism and lived imperfectly in a life that "reads" Scripture, they are the reality of the resurrection that comes the other side of death. There is an analogy, I am saying, between the life of God projected on the screen of human history (the Incarnation) and the life of believers, a life for now (but not for ever) "hid with Christ in God" (Col. 3.3).

That analogy subverts any residue of individualist separateness that we might try to import into heaven. Heaven is not "me and God," not "me and Jesus"; nor is it "me and all the other pretty decent people who can learn to exist alongside each other." Heaven is the realm of the Holy Spirit, the realm, that is, of true communications. Yes, the Holy Spirit is the love, the will, the joy of God in himself; but it is no stretch to refer to the loving, joyful, perfect actualization of the will as "true communications." We know and are known perfectly (as Paul puts it, "then shall I know even as also I am known" [1 Cor. 13.12]). It becomes true at last that each of us linguistic animals is the mode in which society realizes itself. McCabe, as we have seen, calls this the linguistic revolution. The whole precedes the part, and in the individual the whole comes to actualization. This is literally true in heaven, where there is no impingement upon communication. We cannot import into this picture any separatist individuality. We cannot, thus, conceive the inhabitants of heaven as in any way separated from each other. The identity of each entails the flourishing of all; the identity of all allows the actualization of each.

What this means for authority cannot be imagined. We can see its necessity, given by the immensely complicated matter of deciding amongst an ever-increasing world of possible good things to do. We can see, too, that heaven is *interesting*. The fallacy of the old canard, "I'd choose heaven for the climate, hell for the company," is exposed. There is nothing interesting in disease, small-mindedness, or individuals who want only to be alone. Creativity is interesting, the play of language, the invention of new things, the discovery of unexpected worlds now open to our (yes, only) apprehending. Human beings, ensouled bodies, free from sin and death, living together in unimpeded communications—this is what heaven is. If you want to put it simply, just say, Heaven is friends living together.

But they are not at rest. They are active beyond our imagination. And they are so, thanks to authority.

BIBLIOGRAPHY

Apart from versions of the Bible, standard editions of the Book of Common Prayer, and classical works of Aristotle, Augustine, and Thomas Aquinas, the following list is comprehensive of all works mentioned in the text or notes above.

Abbot, Walter M., ed. *The Documents of Vatican II.* New York: Guild Press, 1966.

Adler, Mortimer. *How to Think About God.* New York: Macmillan, 1980.

Anglican-Roman Catholic International Commission. *Authority in the Church III: The Gift of Authority.* 1999. On Centro Pro Unione website: http://www.prounione.urbe.it/dia-int/arcic/doc/e_arcicII_05.html.

— *The Final Report.* London: SPCK and Catholic Truth Society, 1982.

Arendt, Hanna. *Between Past and Future.* New ed. New York: Viking Press, 1968.

Austin, Victor Lee. "A Christological Social Vision: The Uses of Christ in the Social Encyclicals of John Paul II." Ph.D. dissertation. Fordham University, 2002.

— "Is There an Anglican Method in Theology? Hints from the *Lux Mundi* Era." *Sewanee Theological Review* 42 (1999): 290–310.

— "John Paul II's Ironic Legacy in Political Theology." *Pro Ecclesia* 16 (2007): 165–94.

Bach, J. S. *Matthäus Passion.* Trans. Choral Society of Durham, N.Car., in Saint Thomas Choir program. New York: Saint Thomas Church, 2009.

Bartholomew, Craig, et al., eds. *A Royal Priesthood? The Use of the Bible Ethically and Politically: A Dialogue with Oliver O'Donovan.* Carlisle, Cumbria, UK: Paternoster, and Grand Rapids, Mich.: Zondorvan, 2002.

Bauerschmidt, Frederick Christian. *Holy Teaching: Introducing the* Summa Theologiae *of St. Thomas Aquinas.* Grand Rapids, Mich.: Brazos Press, 2005.

Bellah, Robert N. "Freedom, Coercion, and Authority." *Academe*, January/February, 1999, FindArticles.com, October 11, 2007.

Booty, John E., ed. *The Book of Common Prayer 1559: The Elizabethan Prayer Book.* Charlottesville, Va.: The University Press of Virginia, for the Folger Shakespeare Library, 1976.

Buchanan, Scott. *So Reason Can Rule.* New York: Farrar, Straus, Giroux, 1982.

Cavanaugh, T. A. *Double-Effect Reasoning: Doing Good and Avoiding Evil.* Oxford: Clarendon Press, 2006.

Childress, James F. *Civil Disobedience and Political Obligation: A Study in Christian Social Ethics.* New Haven: Yale University Press, 1971.

Dante Alighieri. *Paradiso.* Trans. Robert and Jean Hollander. New York: Doubleday, 2007.

— *Paradiso.* Trans. P. H. Wicksteed. London: J. M. Dent and Sons, 1965.

Davies, Brian. *The Reality of God and the Problem of Evil.* London: Continuum, 2006.

Dulles, Avery. *Church and Society: The Laurence J. McGinley Lectures, 1988–2007.* New York: Fordham University Press, 2008.

— *The Craft of Theology: From Symbol to System.* Expanded ed. New York: Crossroad, 1995.

— *Models of the Church.* Expanded ed. New York: Doubleday, 1987.

Eliot, T. S. *Four Quartets.* New York: Harcourt Brace Jovanovich, 1971.

Farrow, Douglas. *Ascension and Ecclesia: On the Significance of the Doctrine of the Ascension for Ecclesiology and Christian Cosmology.* Grand Rapids, Mich.: Eerdmans, 1999.

Fitzmyer, Joseph A. *The Gospel According to Luke.* The Anchor Bible. Garden City, N.Y.: Doubleday, 1985.

Flannery, Kevin L. *Acts Amid Precepts.* Washington, D.C.: Catholic University of America Press, 2001.

Gelwick, Richard. *The Way of Discovery: An Introduction to the Thought of Michael Polanyi.* New York: Oxford University Press, 1977.

Gill, Jerry H. *The Tacit Mode: Michael Polanyi's Postmodern Philosophy.* Albany: State University of New York Press, 2000.

Gundry, Robert H. *Mark: A Commentary on His Apology for the Cross.* Grand Rapids, Mich.: Eerdmans, 1993.

Gutiérrez, Gustavo. *A Theology of Liberation.* Rev. ed. Maryknoll, N.Y.: Orbis, 1988.

Hamburger, Philip. *Separation of Church and State.* Cambridge, Mass.: Harvard University Press, 2002.

Harris, R. Baine, ed. *Authority: A Philosophical Analysis.* Alabama: University of Alabama Press, 1976.

Hooker, Richard. *Of the Laws of Ecclesiastical Polity*. Ed. John Keble, 3rd ed. Oxford: Oxford University Press, 1845.

Jenson, Robert W. *Systematic Theology*. Vol. 1, *The Triune God*. Oxford: Oxford University Press, 1997.

— *Thinking the Human: Resolutions of Difficult Notions*. Grand Rapids, Mich.: Eerdmans, 2003.

Kennedy, Eugene, and Sara C. Charles. *Authority: The Most Misunderstood Idea in America*. New York: The Free Press, 1997.

Kittel, Gerhard. *Theological Dictionary of the New Testament*. Trans. Geoffrey W. Bromiley. Grand Rapids, Mich.: Eerdmans, 1964–76.

Kuhn, Thomas S. *The Copernican Revolution: Planetary Astronomy in the Development of Western Thought*. Cambridge, Mass.: Harvard University Press, 1957.

Kuic, Vukan. *Yves R. Simon: Real Democracy*. Lanham, Md.: Roman & Littlefield, 1999.

Lewis, C. S. *The Great Divorce*. New York: Macmillan, 1946. Repr. New York: HarperCollins, 2001.

MacDougal, Gary. *Make a Difference*. New York: St. Martin's Press, 2005.

MacIntyre, Alisdair. *After Virtue*. 3rd ed. Notre Dame: University of Notre Dame Press, 2007.

Marshall, Paul V. *Prayer Book Parallels: The Public Services of the Church Arranged for Comparative Study*. Anglican Liturgy in America, vol. 1. New York: Church Hymnal Corporation, 1989.

McCabe, Herbert. *God Matters*. London: Geoffrey Chapman, 1987. Repr. London: Continuum, 2005.

— *God Still Matters*. London: Continuum, 2002.

— *The Good Life*. London: Continuum, 2005.

Mitchell, Mark T. *Michael Polanyi*. Wilmington, Del.: ISI, 2006.

Moleski, Martin X. *Personal Catholicism: The Theological Epistemologies of John Henry Newman and Michael Polanyi*. Washington, D.C.: Catholic University of America Press, 2000.

Novogratz, Jacqueline. *The Blue Sweater: Bridging the Gap Between Rich and Poor in an Interconnected World*. New York: Rodale Books, 2009.

O'Donovan, Oliver. *Church in Crisis: The Gay Controversy and the Anglican Communion*. Eugene, Ore.: Cascade Books, 2008.

— *The Desire of the Nations*. Cambridge: University of Cambridge Press, 1996.

— *The Just War Revisited*. Cambridge: Cambridge University Press, 2003.

— *Resurrection and Moral Order*. Leicester, England: Inter-Varsity Press; and Grand Rapids, Mich.: Eerdmans, 1986. 2nd ed. Leicester, England: Apollos; and Grand Rapids, Mich.: Eerdmans, 1994.

O'Donovan, Oliver. *The Ways of Judgment.* Grand Rapids, Mich.: Eerdmans, 2005.

O'Donovan, Oliver, and Joan Lockwood O'Donovan. *Bonds of Imperfection.* Grand Rapids, Mich.: Eerdmans, 2004.

O'Donovan, Oliver, and Joan Lockwood O'Donovan, eds. *From Irenaeus to Grotius: A Sourcebook in Christian Political Thought.* Grand Rapids, Mich.: Eerdmans, 1999.

Pius XI. *Quas primas.* 1925. In Claudia Carlen, ed. *The Papal Encyclicals (1740–1981).* Wilmington, N.C.: McGrath, 1981.

Polanyi, Michael. *Knowing and Being: Essays by Michael Polanyi.* Ed. Marjorie Grene. Chicago: University of Chicago Press, 1969.

— *The Logic of Liberty.* Chicago: University of Chicago Press, 1951.

— *Personal Knowledge: Towards a Post-Critical Philosophy.* Chicago: University of Chicago Press, 1958. Corrected ed. Chicago: University of Chicago Press, 1962.

— *The Study of Man.* Chicago: University of Chicago Press, 1959.

— *The Tacit Dimension.* Garden City, N.Y.: Doubleday, 1966.

Polkinghorne, John. *The Faith of a Physicist.* Minneapolis, Minn.: Fortress, 1996.

— *Science and Theology: An Introduction.* London: SPCK, 1998.

Prosch, Harry. *Michael Polanyi: A Critical Exposition.* Albany: State University of New York Press, 1986.

Ptolemy, Copernicus, Kepler. Vol. 16 of *Great Books of the Western World.* Chicago: Encyclopedia Britannica, 1952.

Quinton, Anthony. *The Politics of Imperfection: The Religious and Secular Traditions of Conservative Thought in England from Hooker to Oakeshott.* London: Faber and Faber, 1978.

Radner, Ephraim, and Philip Turner. *The Fate of Communion: The Agony of Anglicanism and the Future of a Global Church.* Grand Rapids, Mich.: Eerdmans, 2006.

Ramsey, Paul. *The Just War.* New York: Charles Scribner's Sons, 1968.

— *War and the Christian Conscience.* Durham, N.C.: Duke University Press, 1961.

Ratzinger, Joseph. *Eschatology: Death and Eternal Life.* Trans. Michael Waldstein and Aidan Nichols. Washington, D.C.: Catholic University of America Press, 1988.

Rawls, John. *A Theory of Justice.* Cambridge, Mass.: Harvard University Press, 1971.

Raz, Joseph, ed. *Authority.* New York: New York University Press, 1990.

Rieff, Philip. *Charisma: The Gift of Grace, and How It Has Been Taken Away from Us.* New York: Pantheon Books, 2007.

Scott, Drusilla. *Everyman Revisited: The Common Sense of Michael Polanyi.* Grand Rapids, Mich.: Eerdmans, 1995.

Seitz, Christopher R., ed. *Nicene Christianity.* Grand Rapids, Mich.: Brazos Press, 2001.

Selwyn, Edward Gordon, ed. *Essays Catholic and Critical.* 3rd ed. London: Society for Promoting Christian Knowledge, 1929.

Simon, Anthony O., ed. *Acquaintance with the Absolute: The Philosophy of Yves R. Simon.* New York: Fordham University Press, 1998.

Simon, Yves R. *Freedom of Choice.* New York: Fordham University Press, 1969.

— *A General Theory of Authority.* Notre Dame: University of Notre Dame Press, 1962; repr. 1980.

— *Introduction to the Metaphysics of Knowledge.* Trans. Vukan Kuic and Richard J. Thompson. New York: Fordham University Press, 1990.

— *Nature and Functions of Authority.* Milwaukee: Marquette University Press, 1940; repr. 1948.

— *Philosophy of Democratic Government.* Chicago: University of Chicago Press, 1951. Rev. ed. Notre Dame: University of Notre Dame Press, 1993.

Stout, Jeffrey. *The Flight from Authority: Religion, Morality, and the Quest for Autonomy.* Notre Dame: University of Notre Dame Press, 1981.

Sykes, Stephen. *Power and Christian Theology.* London: Continuum, 2006.

Tanner, Mary. "The ARCIC Dialogue and the Perception of Authority." *Journal of Anglican Studies* 1.2 (2003): 47–61.

Thielicke, Helmut. *Theological Ethics.* Vol. 2, *Politics.* Grand Rapids, Mich.: Eerdmans, 1979.

Torre, Michael D., ed. *Freedom in the Modern World: Jacques Maritain, Yves R. Simon, Mortimer J. Adler.* Mishawaka, Ind.: American Maritain Association, 1989.

Turner, Philip Williams, III. "Theological Anthropology and the State: A Study of the Political Ethics of Yves Simon and Helmut Thielicke." Ph.D. dissertation., Princeton University, 1978.

Wainwright, Geoffrey, ed. *Keeping the Faith: Essays to Mark the Centenary of "Lux Mundi."* Philadelphia: Fortress, 1988.

Wright, N. T. *Surprised by Hope: Rethinking Heaven, the Resurrection, and the Mission of the Church.* New York: HarperOne, 2008.

INDEX OF SCRIPTURAL CITATIONS

INDEX OF SUBJECTS

In conjunction with the following index, the reader should consult the table of contents on pages vii–viii. It will guide the reader to the major discussions of social, epistemic, political, and ecclesial authority, the misfirings of authority, and the place of authority in paradise.